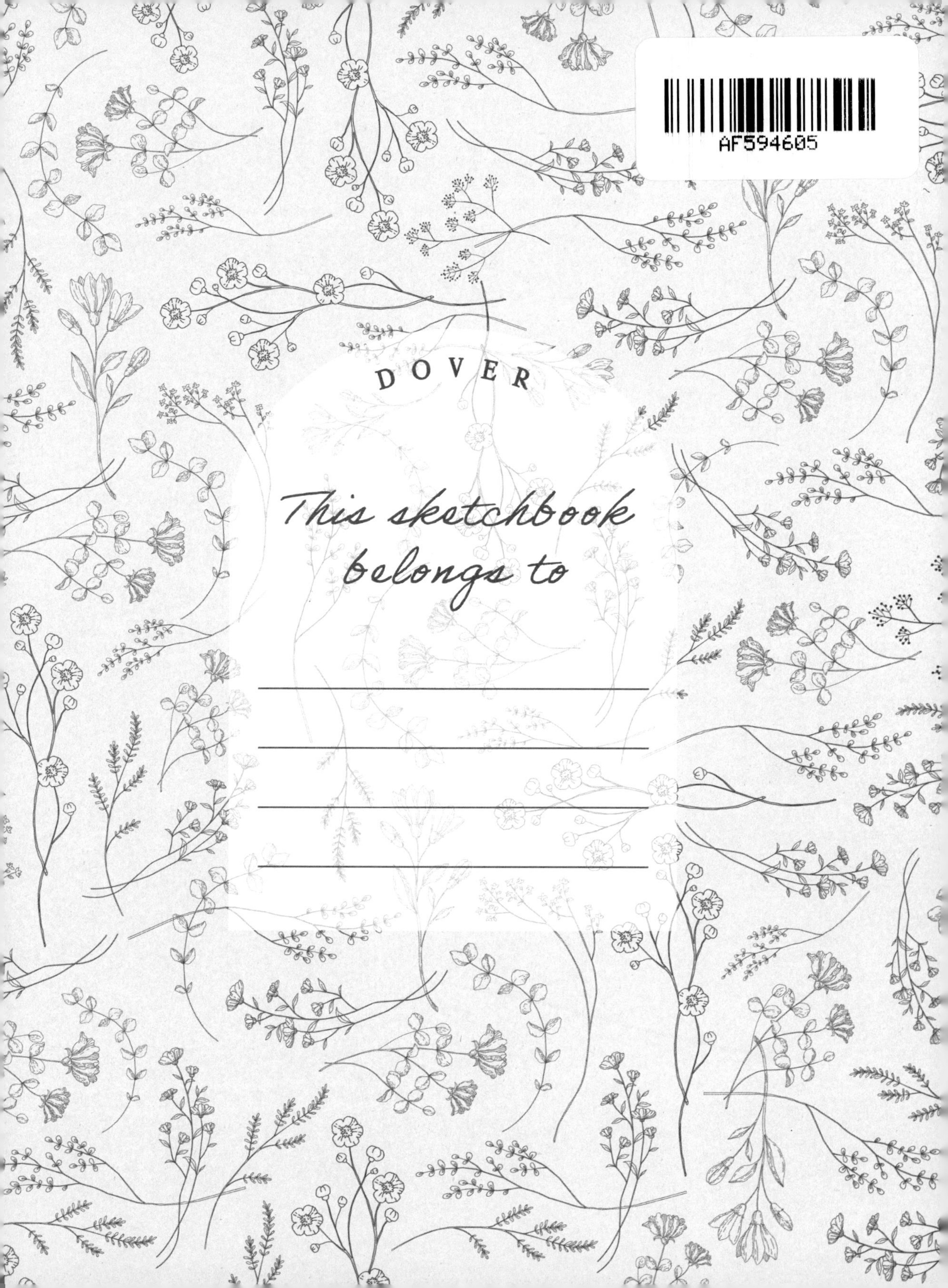

AF594605
DOVER
This sketchbook belongs to

Nature Drawing: Trees: A Guided Sketchbook with Prompts & Tips from the Pros is a new work, first published by Dover Publications in 2025.

ISBN-13: 978-0-486-85408-3
ISBN-10: 0-486-85408-6

Publisher: Betina Cochran
Acquisitions Editor: Allyson D'Antonio
Managing Editorial Supervisor: Susan Rattiner
Production Editor: Gregory Koutrouby
Editorial, Design, and Layout: Elizabeth T. Gilbert and Coffee Cup Creative LLC
Creative Manager: Marie Zaczkiewicz
Production: Pam Weston, Tammi McKenna, Ayse Yilmaz

Printed in China
85408601 2025
www.doverpublications.com

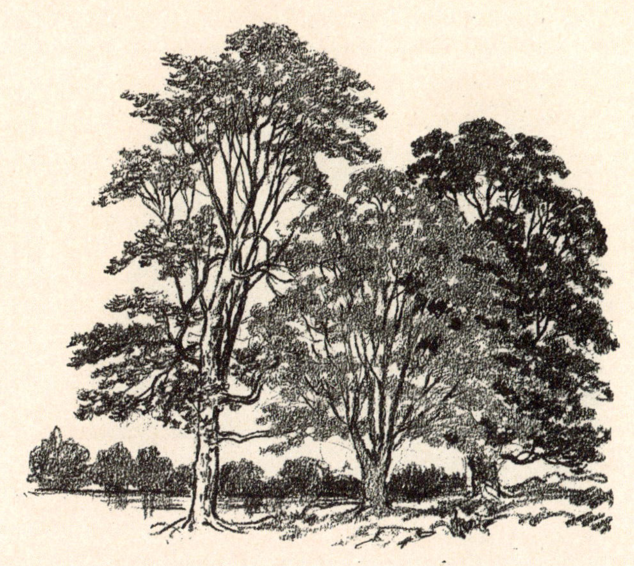

NATURE DRAWING

Trees

A GUIDED SKETCHBOOK
WITH PROMPTS & TIPS
FROM THE PROS

Victor Perard

Dover Publications
Garden City, New York

TABLE OF CONTENTS

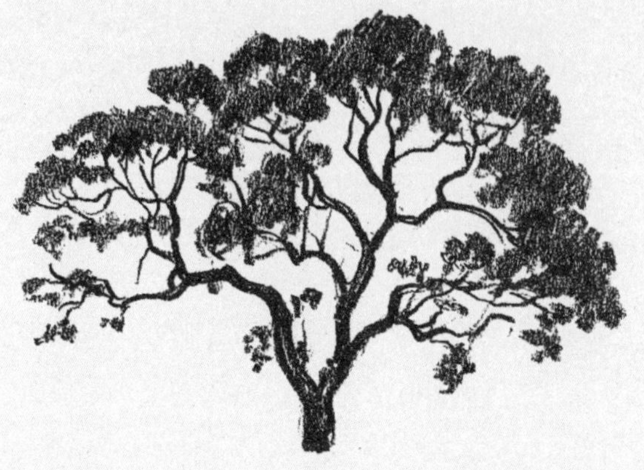

INTRODUCTION

Learning to capture the essence of nature in a drawing is one of the most rewarding experiences available to an artist. Sketching is not just a way to copy a scene; it's a way to more clearly see and more deeply understand the wonders around us. Think of sketching as a welcoming and flexible art form that encourages experimentation, develops your observational skills, and allows you to record personal memories.

This guided sketchbook uses the timeless art of Victor Perard to inspire and instruct you as you dive into the art of sketching trees. Simply sketch along inside this book where prompted, and use the pages at the end of this book for recording your own original sketches.

Why I've chosen to begin this sketchbook...

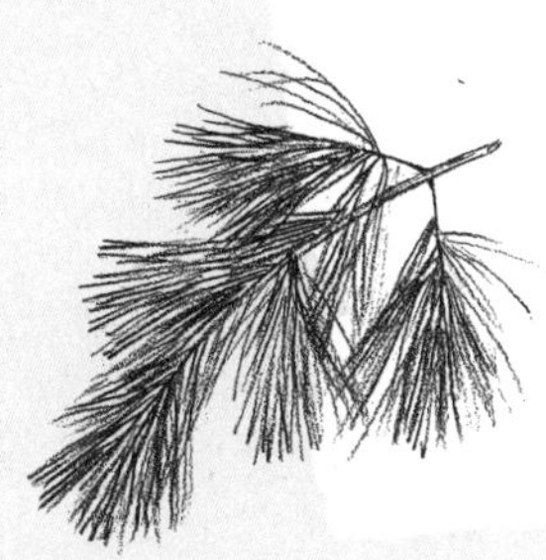

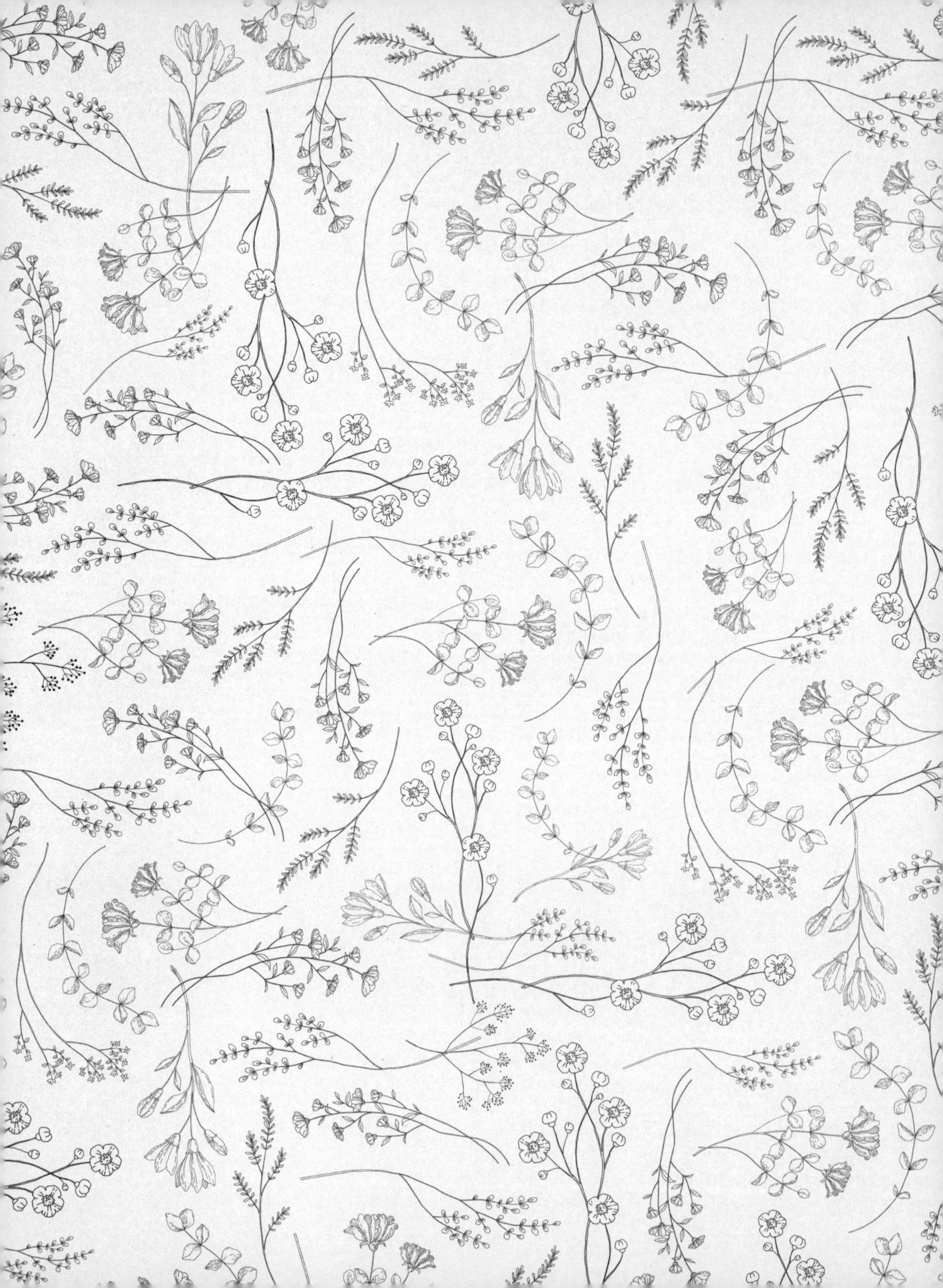

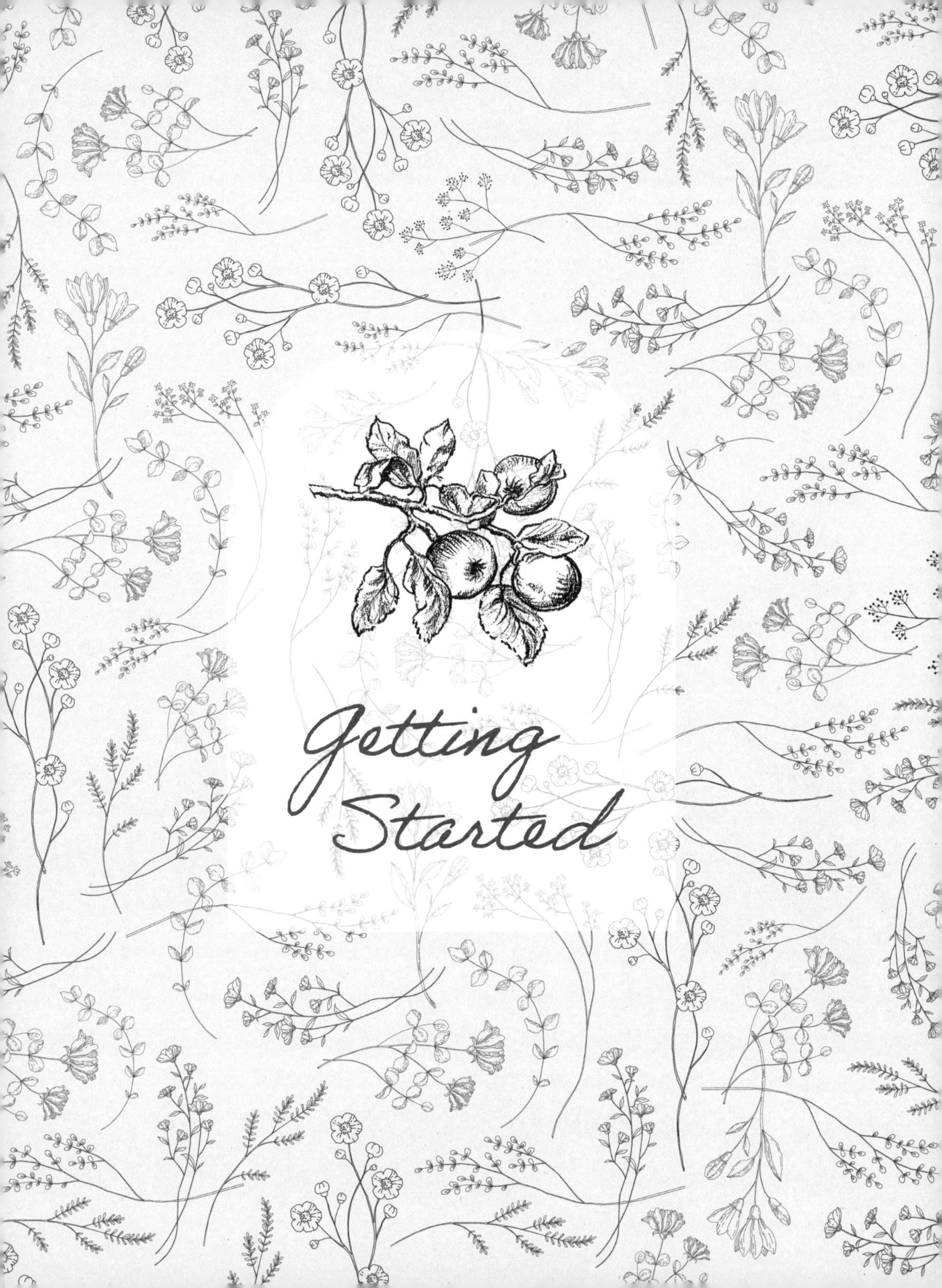

Getting Started

TOOLS & MATERIALS

Pencil drawing is one of the easiest fine arts to master. It requires only a few tools, and cleanup is simple. Moreover, with the help of a small bag or case, pencil drawing is easy to perform on the go and in the presence of your subject. The following pages will help you gather the tools you'll need to get the most out of this sketchbook.

Graphite Pencils

Drawing pencils are generally wood-encased pencils with a graphite lead. Leads are labeled by hardness, ranging from very soft (6B) to medium (HB) to very hard (6H). For landscape sketching, it's a good idea to begin simply with just a few pencils on hand, such as an HB and a soft pencil (2B or 3B).

Sharpeners

Keep a pencil sharpener on hand for maintaining sharp tips. Sharpeners with a small compartment for collecting the shavings are convenient for artists on the go. If you prefer sketching with flat or blunt tips, you can further hone the lead tip using fine sandpaper or a crafting knife.

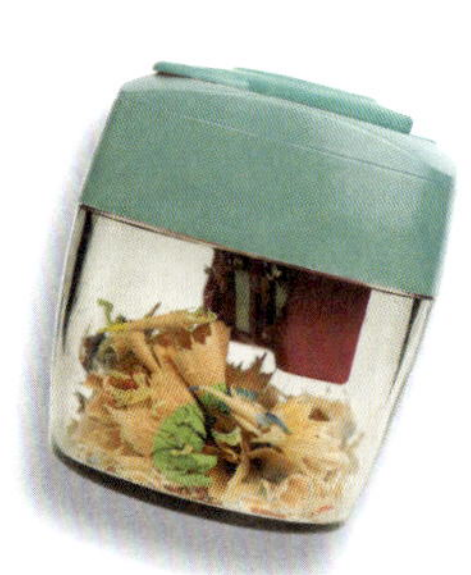

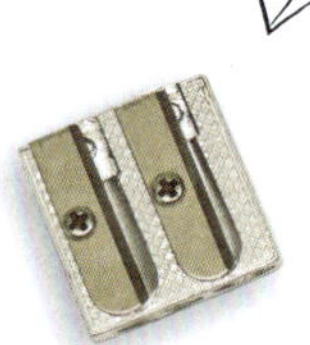

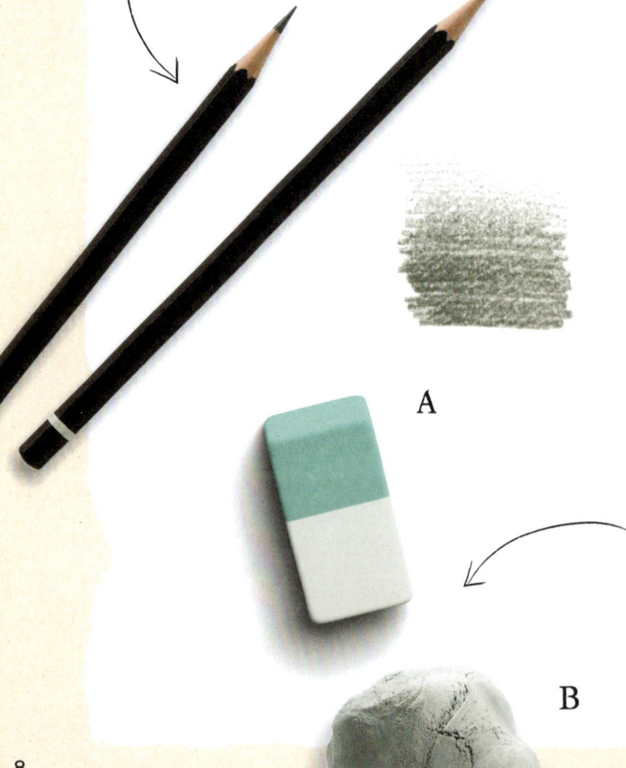

A

B

Erasers

Rubber (A), plastic, gum, and kneaded erasers are all effective in removing graphite from paper. Kneaded erasers (B) are great art tools in themselves. You can use them to gently dab away graphite and subtly lighten tones, or you can shape them into fine points to create detailed highlights.

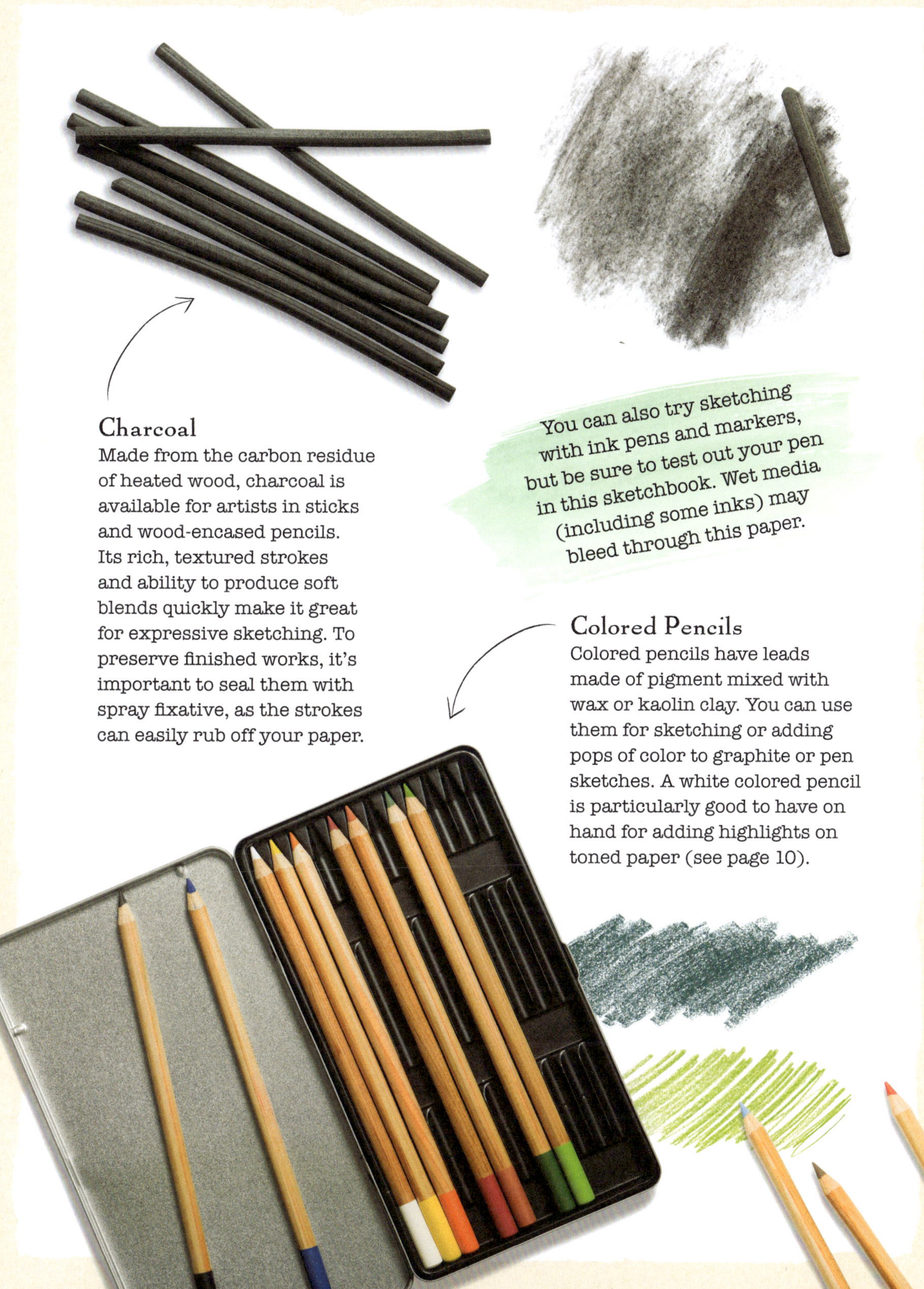

Charcoal

Made from the carbon residue of heated wood, charcoal is available for artists in sticks and wood-encased pencils. Its rich, textured strokes and ability to produce soft blends quickly make it great for expressive sketching. To preserve finished works, it's important to seal them with spray fixative, as the strokes can easily rub off your paper.

You can also try sketching with ink pens and markers, but be sure to test out your pen in this sketchbook. Wet media (including some inks) may bleed through this paper.

Colored Pencils

Colored pencils have leads made of pigment mixed with wax or kaolin clay. You can use them for sketching or adding pops of color to graphite or pen sketches. A white colored pencil is particularly good to have on hand for adding highlights on toned paper (see page 10).

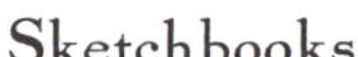

Once you've filled up this book with drawings, you'll want to purchase a sketchbook. These portable drawing pads come in a range of sizes, bindings, and paper types. Choose a format that feels comfortable to you and a paper type that is suitable for your drawing media of choice. Smooth or medium-textured paper is best for graphite, whereas rough or grain-textured paper is ideal for charcoal. A mixed-media sketchbook is a great choice for beginners and experimenters, as this versatile paper will be heavy enough to accept ink.

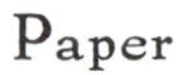

Many artists use their sketchbooks to create preliminary drawings for more polished works of art. For finished art, choose high-quality paper, and consider using spray fixative to set the artwork and prevent your strokes from smudging.

You may also want to experiment with toned paper; use white colored pencil or white charcoal to add dynamic highlights that "pop" from the paper.

WARMING UP

Before you begin sketching, always take some time to warm up and get comfortable with your drawing tools. Perform some simple strokes and exercises to loosen up your wrist and develop control over the pencil, and practice long, broad strokes for shading. The following pages provide samples to guide you through the warm-up process.

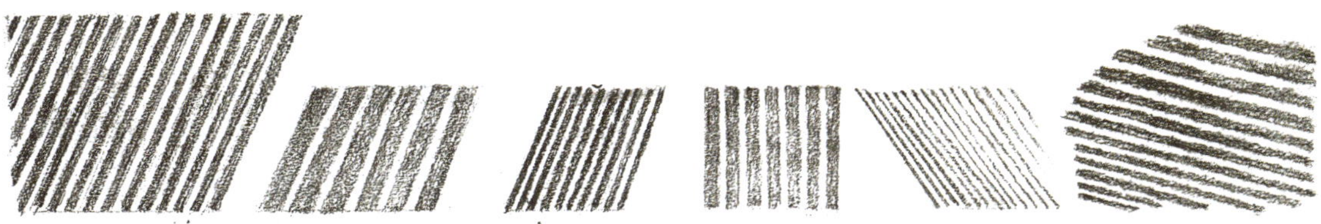

Practice making parallel strokes while keeping their weight and relative distances consistent. Whether you are right- or left-handed, this will prove to be excellent practice for future work while encouraging hand-eye coordination.

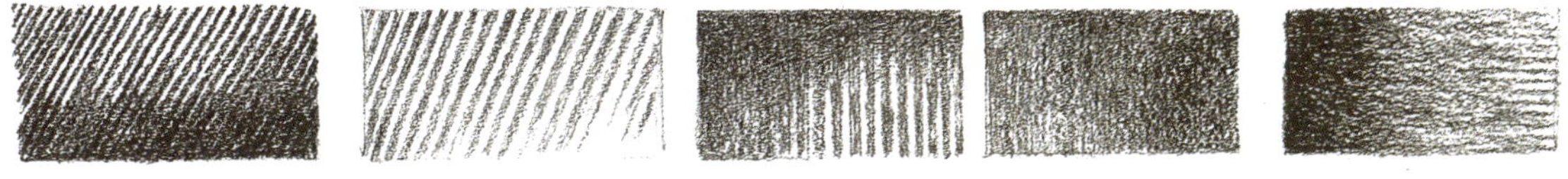

Now keep your lines closer together, melting them into flat and gradated tones, as illustrated above. Practice this shading until proficient in control of the pencil and pressure, thus varying the tones and values.

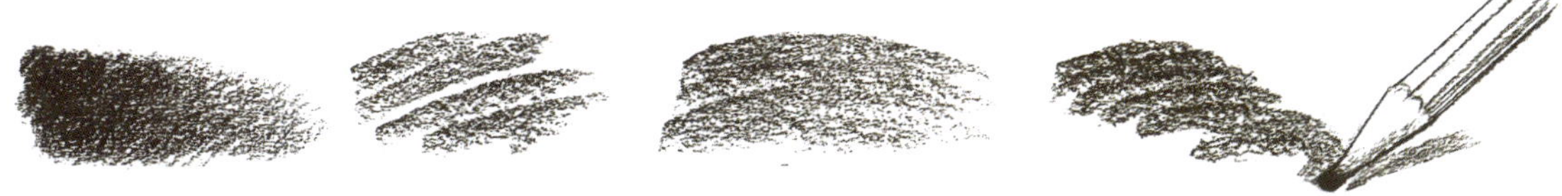

Sharpen the lead of a soft pencil to resemble a chisel, and wear down the lead until smooth for broad strokes. The pencil will then prove practical and effective for sketching. It will help to vary the width of strokes, lending interest to the drawing.

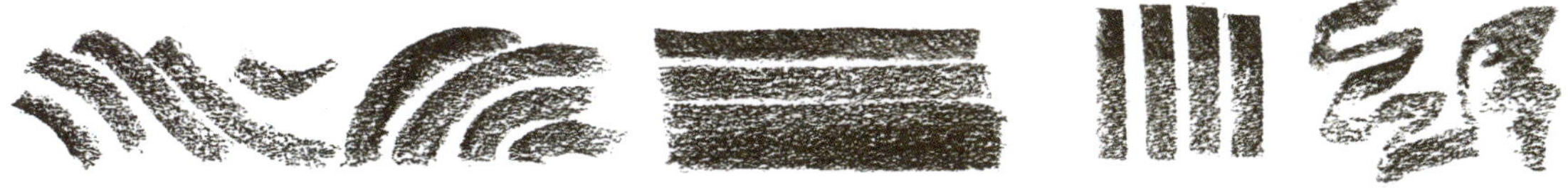

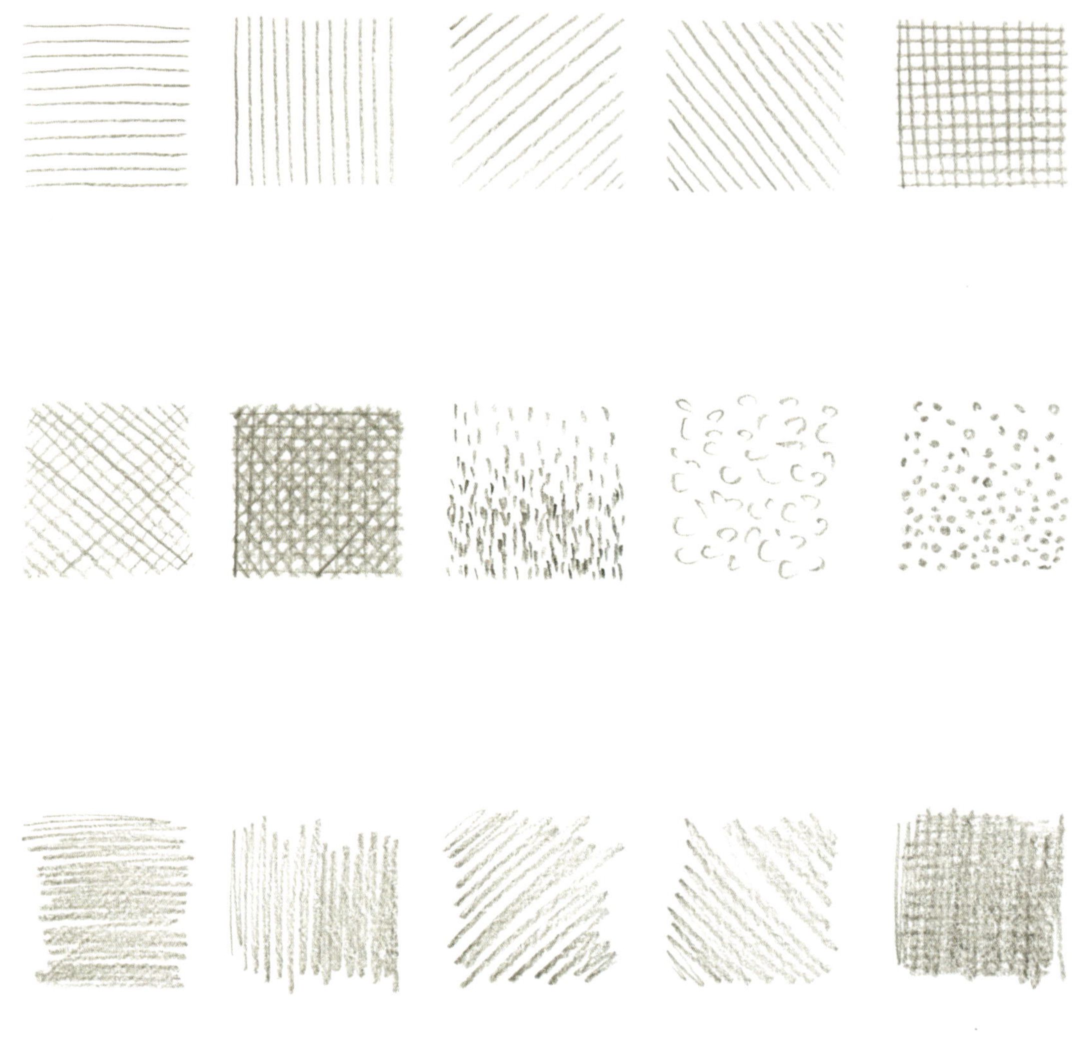

Draw along in this book under each example, or use a separate sheet of scrap paper. You'll be using a variety of marks to describe the character of your trees as you sketch them, so think of this exercise as expanding your "vocabulary" of strokes.

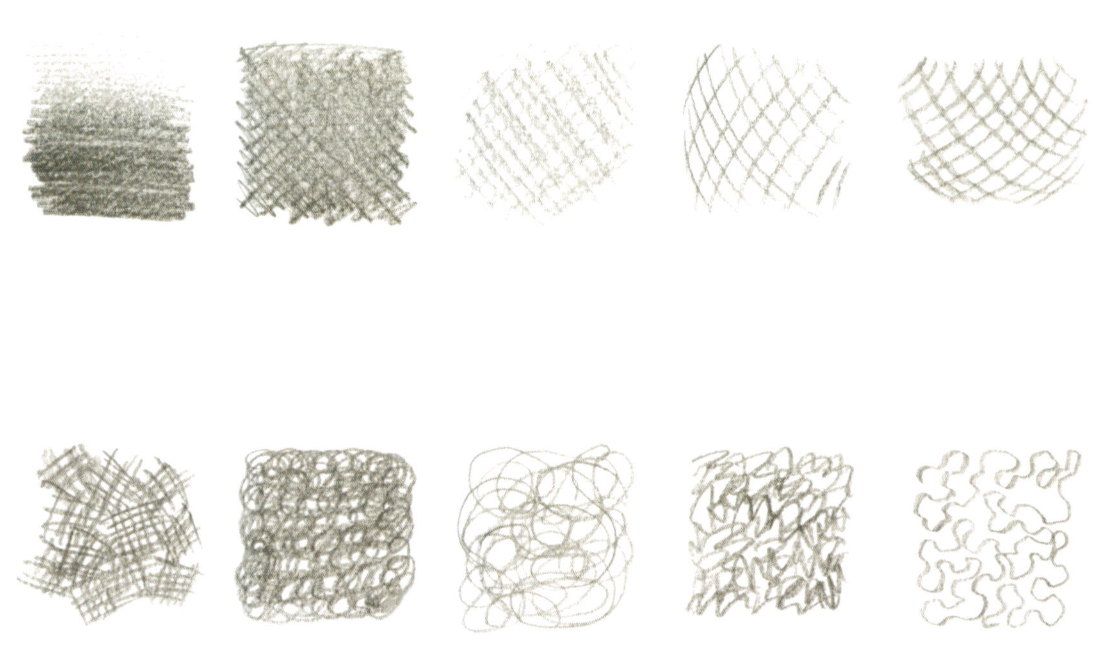

Use this space to experiment with your own strokes. Produce a mix of controlled lines, loose scribbles, hatchmarks, dots, and dashes. Try blending your strokes with tissue for soft gradations.

COMPOSITION

Composition refers to the placement of elements within the edges of your drawing. Good compositions create a pleasing pattern and lead the viewer's eye around the scene. It's a great idea to create small sketches, called "thumbnails," to work out your basic composition before beginning a drawing.

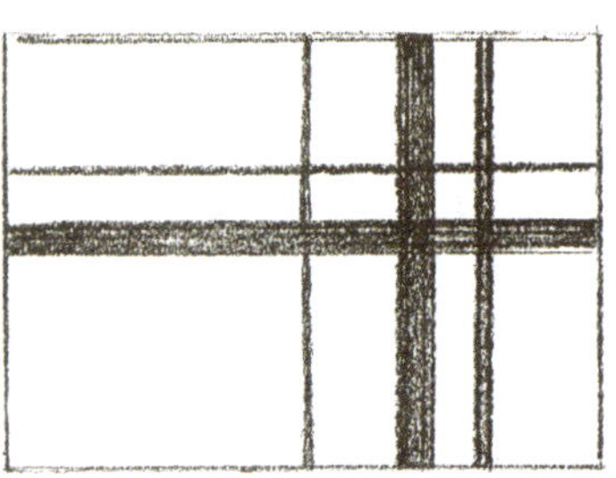

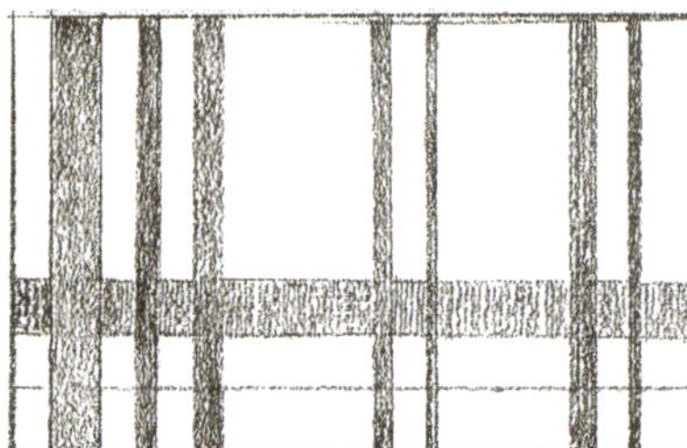

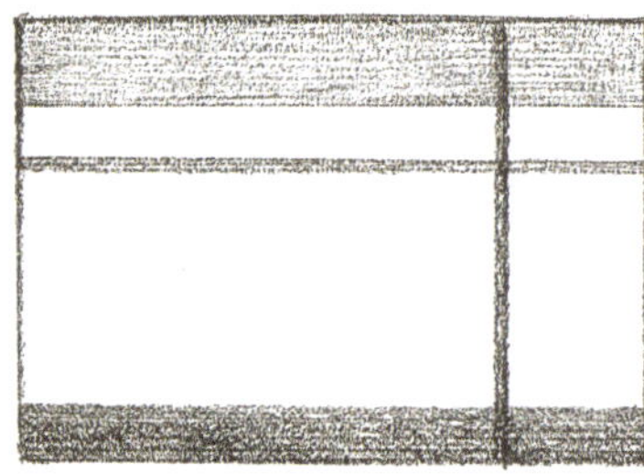

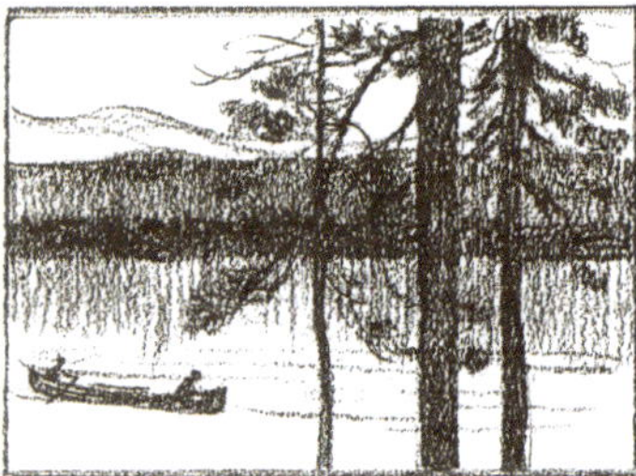

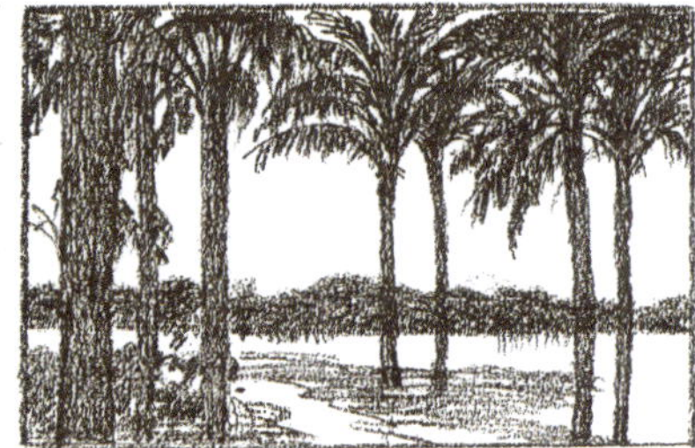

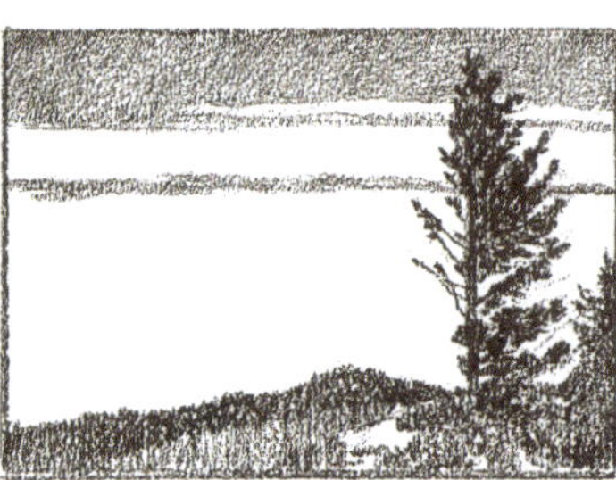

Asymmetry

Avoid placing subjects in the middle of the paper. Instead, consider placing the focal point a third of the way into the composition.

Patterns

The repetition of vertical trunks creates a pleasing rhythm in this beach scene.

Simplicity

Using sparse inclusion and placement of the elements in a scene can communicate peace, vastness, and solitude.

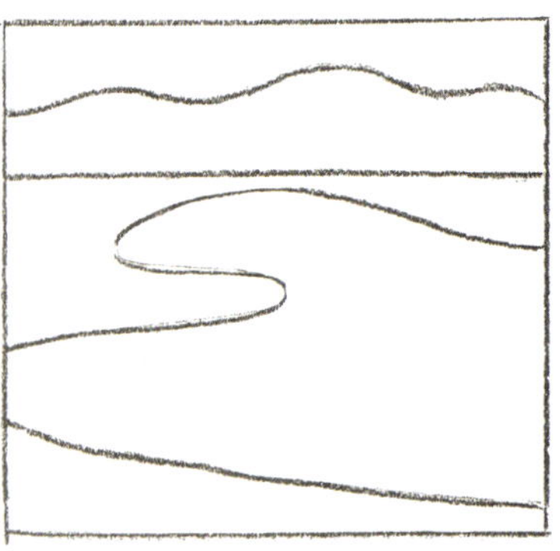

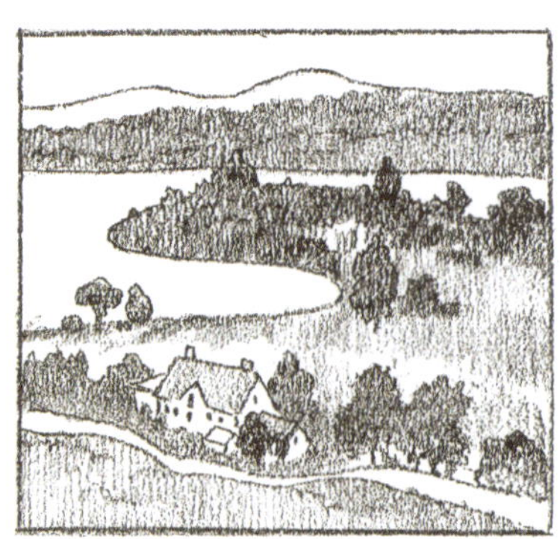

Using Curves

The winding shoreline in this scene leads the eye into and throughout the composition.

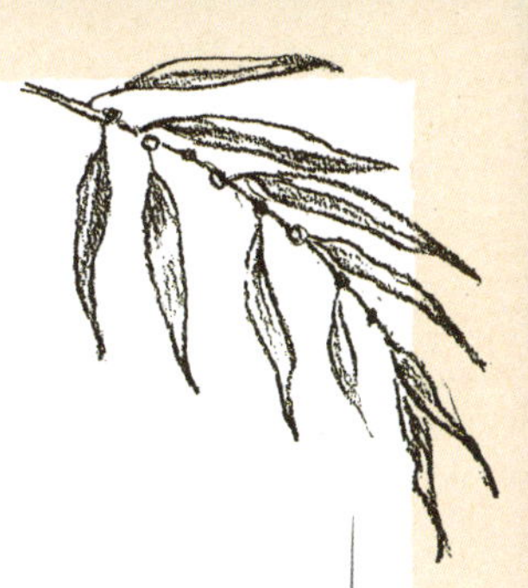

Practice making thumbnail sketches here. Squint your eyes and reduce your scene to its most prominent values and lines. Once you're happy with the composition, sketch it again with more details.

Using Curves

When sketching from nature, it's helpful to make a few viewfinders—a set of cardboard cutouts of various shapes. These windows will help you find a pleasing composition as you scan the scene in front of you.

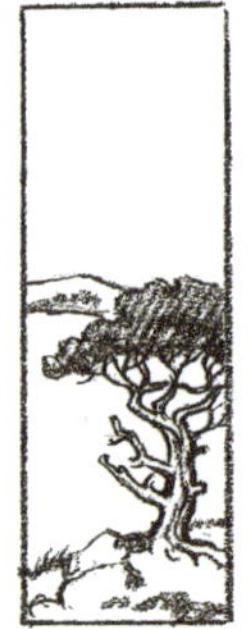

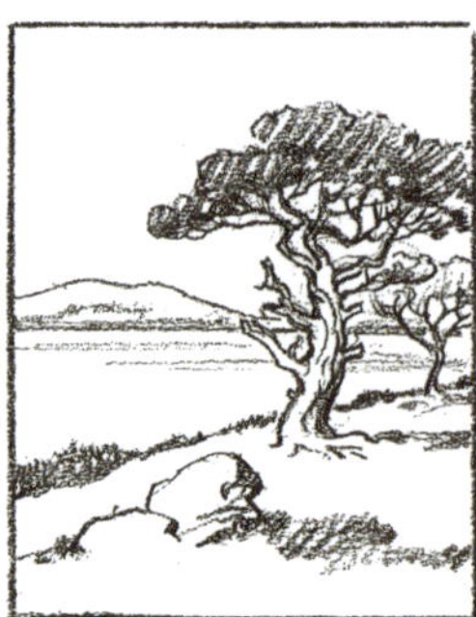

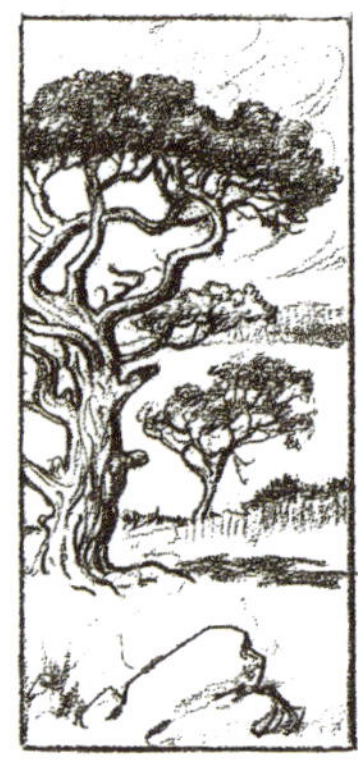

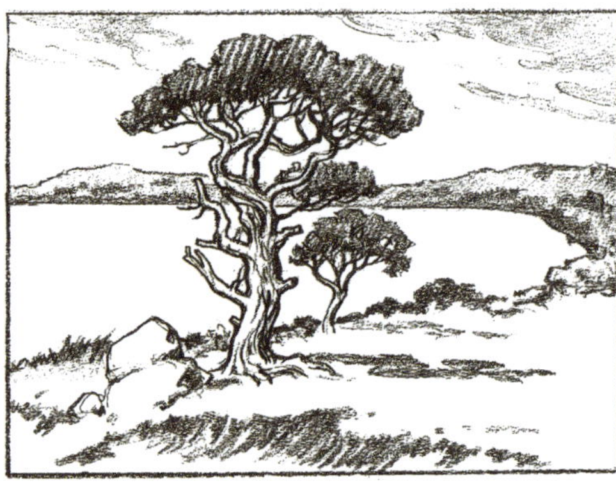

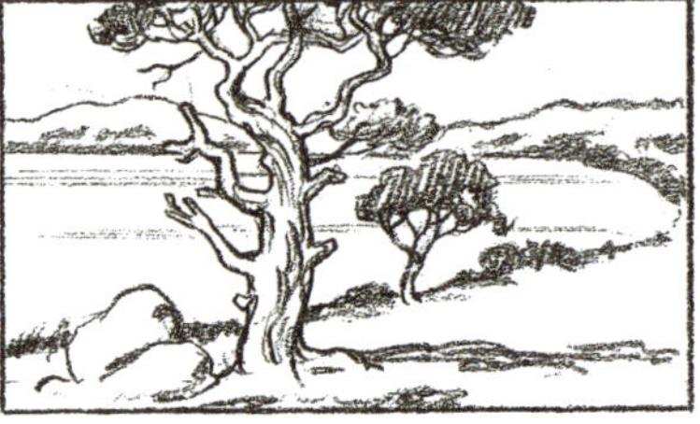

The subjects in these sketches are placed within different-sized borders, illustrating the many possible arrangements that can be obtained from the same subject.

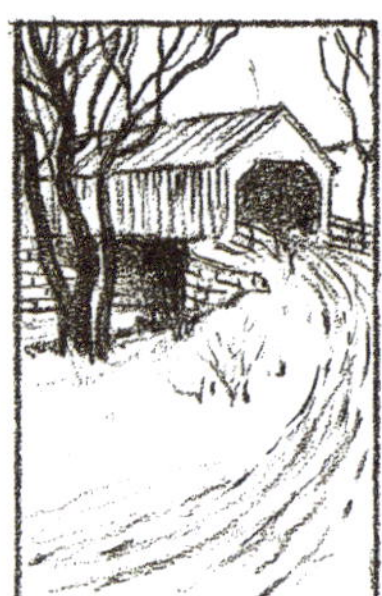

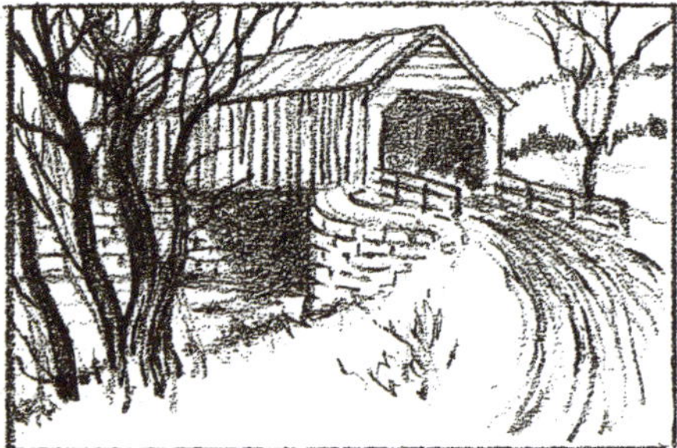

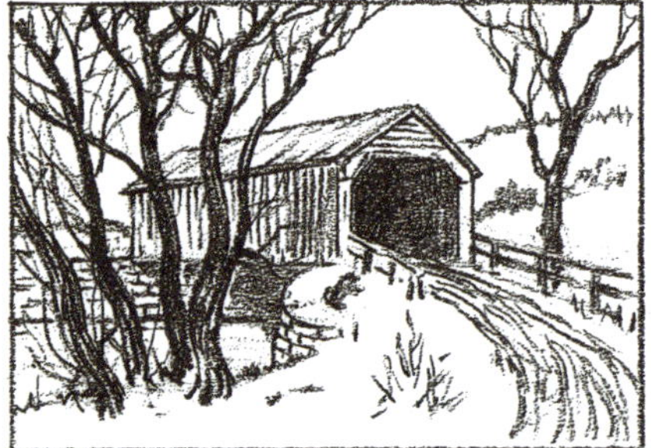

When composing, try sketching the same subject from subtly different viewpoints. Experiment with including more or less foreground in your thumbnails.

A

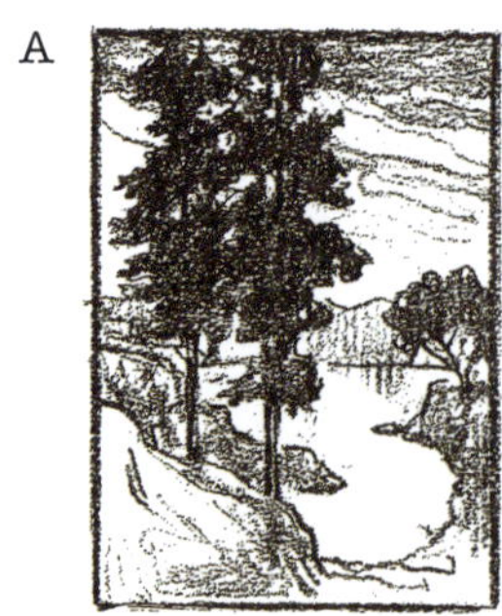

B

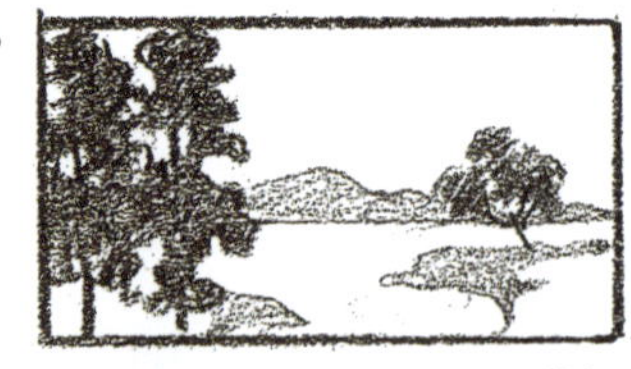

C

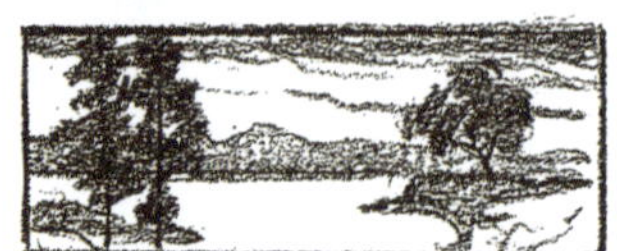

This series at left illustrates the same subject in three common composition formats: vertical (A), horizontal (B), and panoramic (C).

On this page, draw the same scene in several different formats and from a range of different viewpoints. Then select your favorite thumbnail and determine the specific strengths of the composition.

PERSPECTIVE

Perspective is the representation of objects appearing smaller as they become farther from the observer. When the eye is directed to any scene in nature, it embraces no more than what most agreeably fills its power of vision without turning the head. The point of sight is always within the picture, and the line of the horizon is always on level with the eye of the observer.

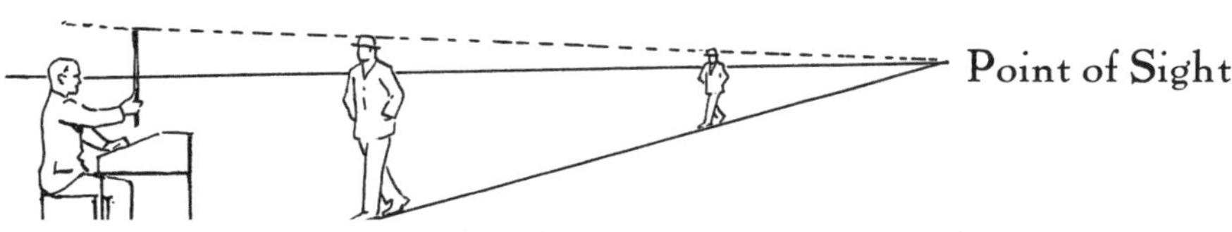

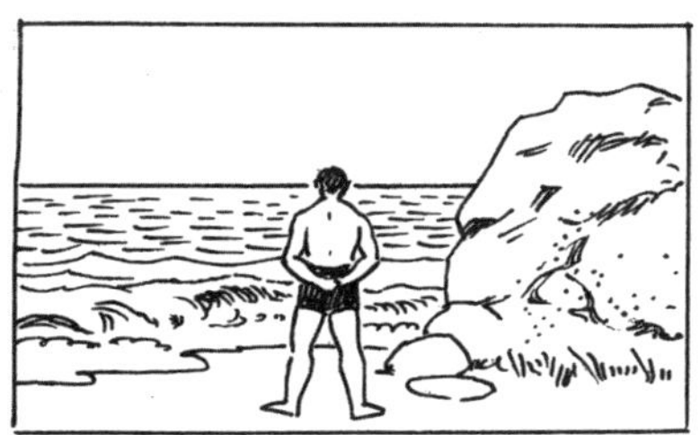

The horizon line is on the level with the eye. The horizon line would have the curve of the earth, but so little of it is seen at a time that it can be drawn straight.

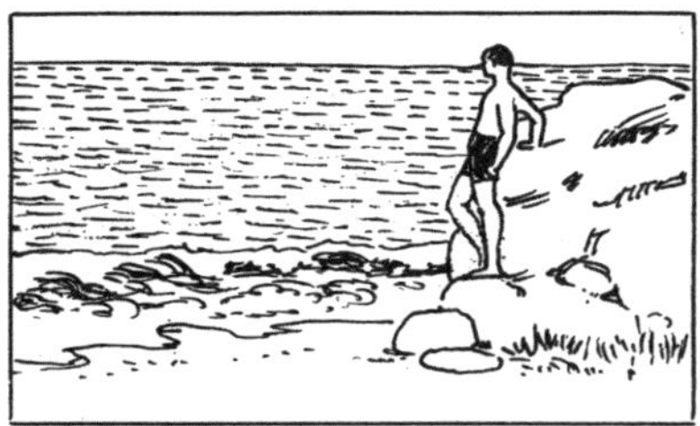

The horizon line is still on a level with the observer's eye, but as he has climbed to a higher level, the horizon line is higher.

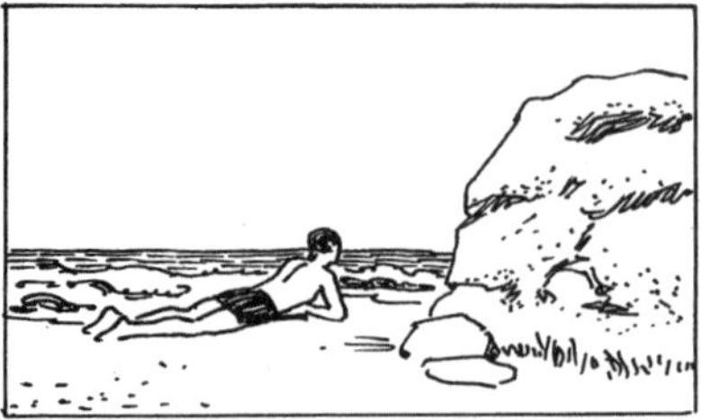

By assuming the onlooker's position, the horizon line is much lower to the eye, as illustrated here.

On this page, draw a scene of your choice, placing the horizon line right at eye level, higher than eye level, and lower than eye level. How does the change in perspective enhance or detract from your art?

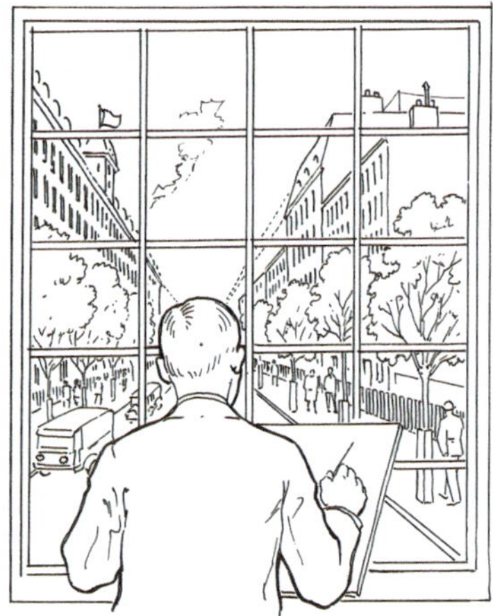

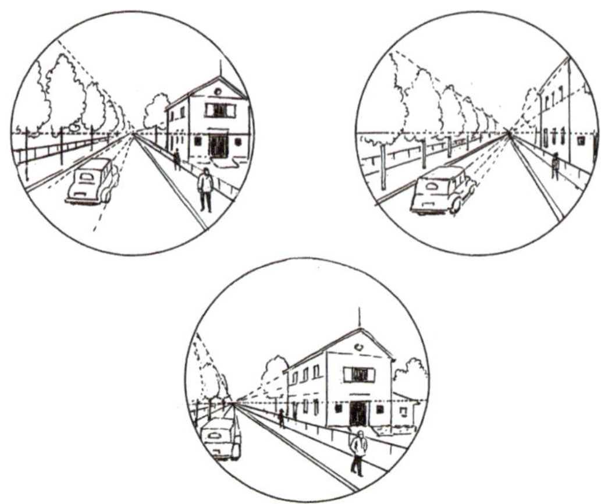

Looking through a window with square panes of glass gives upright lines and horizontal lines to help you see how much of an angle the lines would take to reach the point of sight. To this point of sight, the lines that are parallel converge and end.

The point of sight does not always have to be in the center of the picture. It may suit the composition better to shift it to one side or the other on the horizon line to obtain a more pleasing arrangement.

One-point perspective

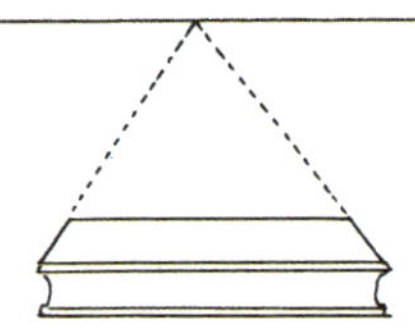

Two-point perspective

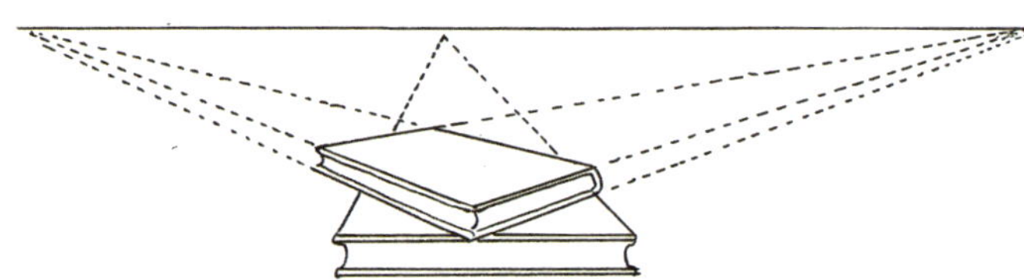

One-point perspective includes one vanishing point, whereas two-point perspective includes two. One-point perspective is best illustrated by a railroad track receding into the distance. Two-point perspective is shown best when viewing a building from the side.

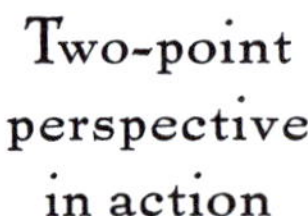

Two-point perspective in action

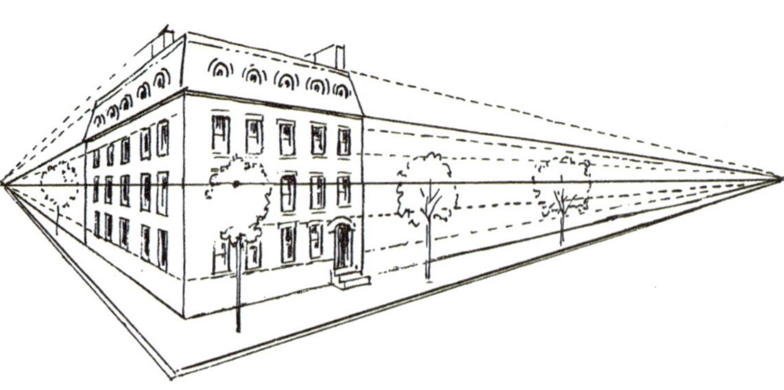

To train your eye to see both one- and two-point perspective, find a long stretch of road that recedes into the distance. Sketch the scene, paying particular attention to the converging lines and how things along the roadside change in size as they become farther away.

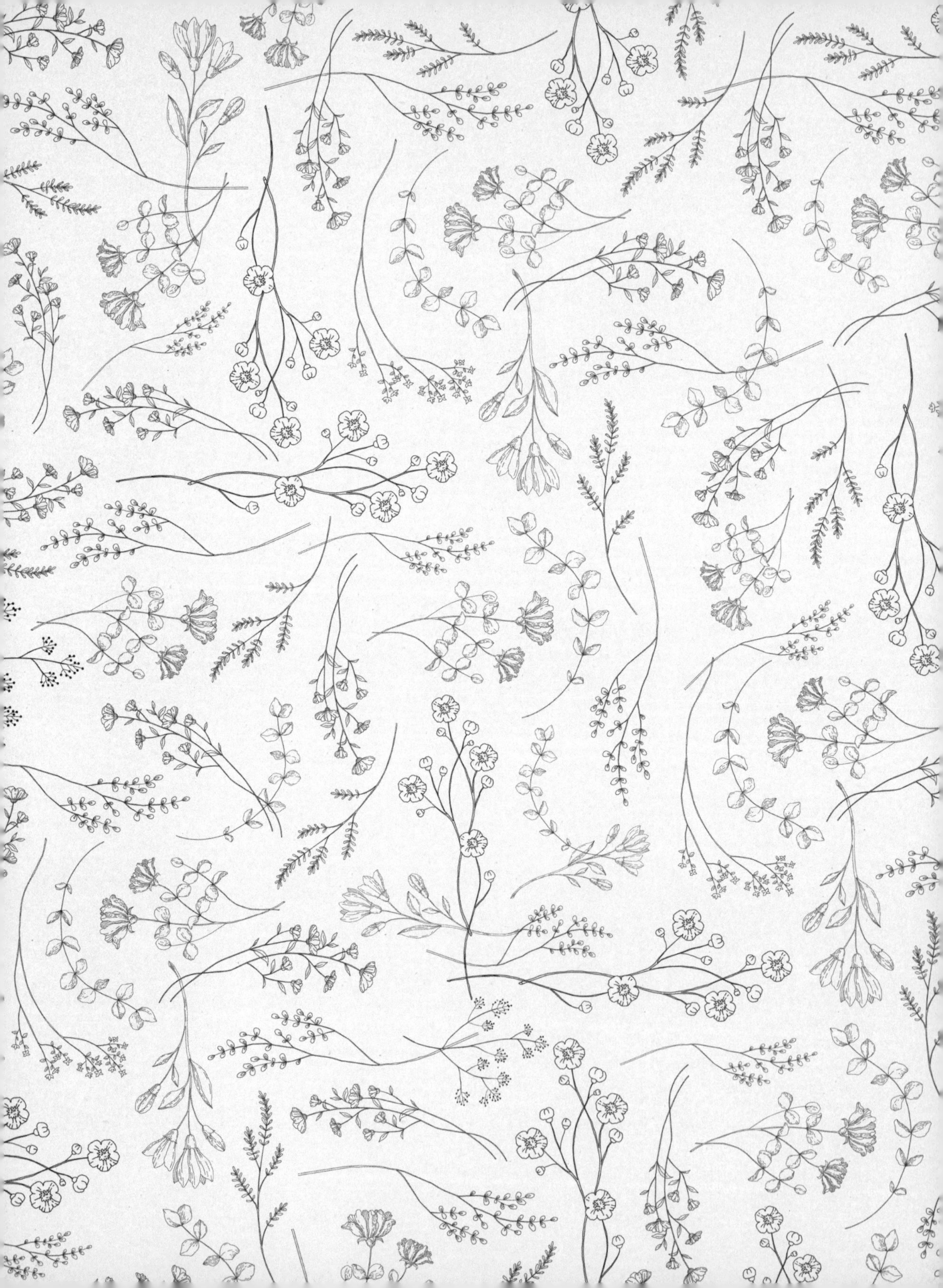

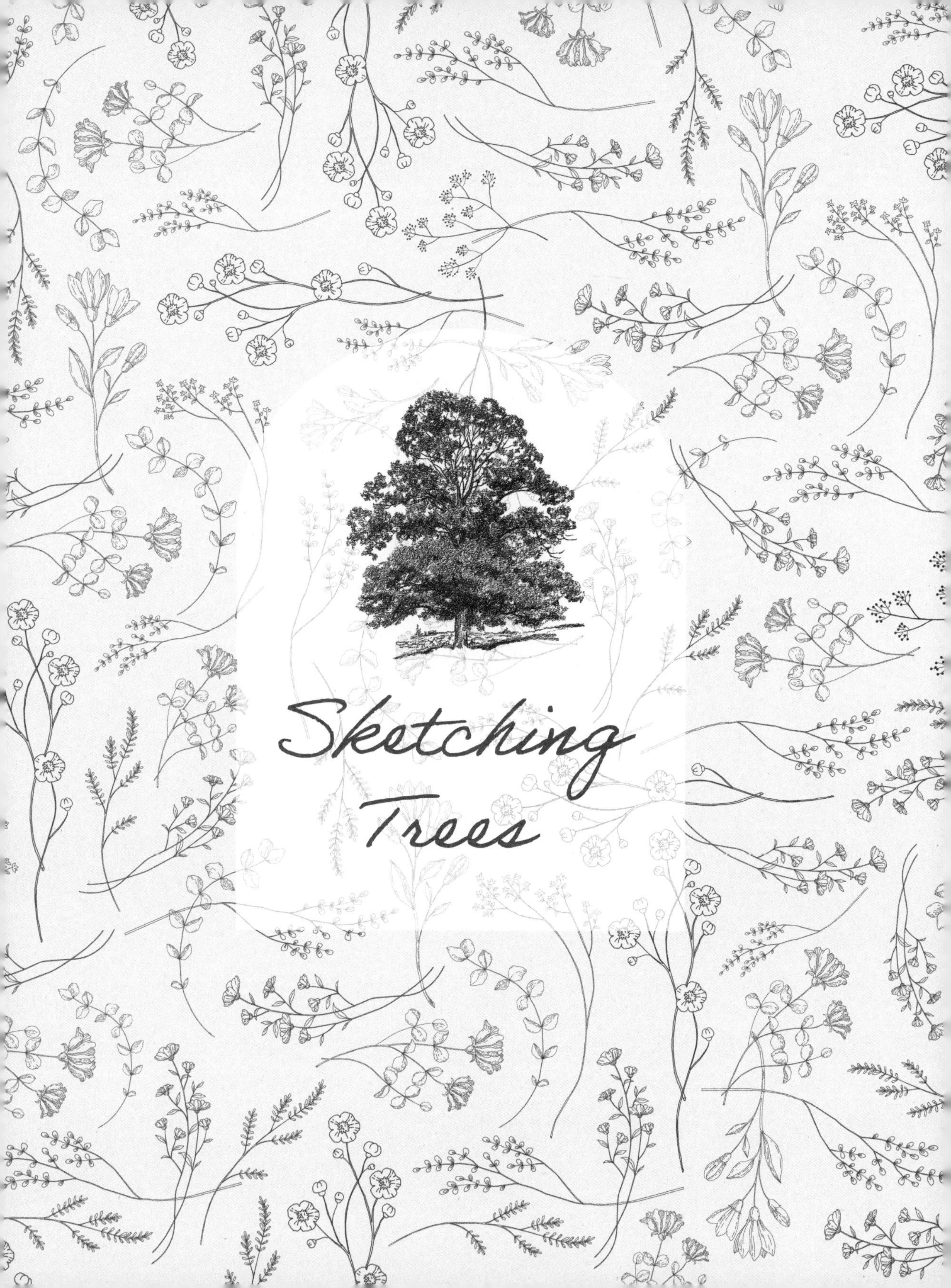
Sketching
Trees

LINEWORK

When trees are reduced to basic lines, their identifying characteristics become more obvious—such as the juniper's flame-like plumes and the elm's perky web of branches and twigs. Draw the simplified forms of various trees to understand their distinct shapes and structures.

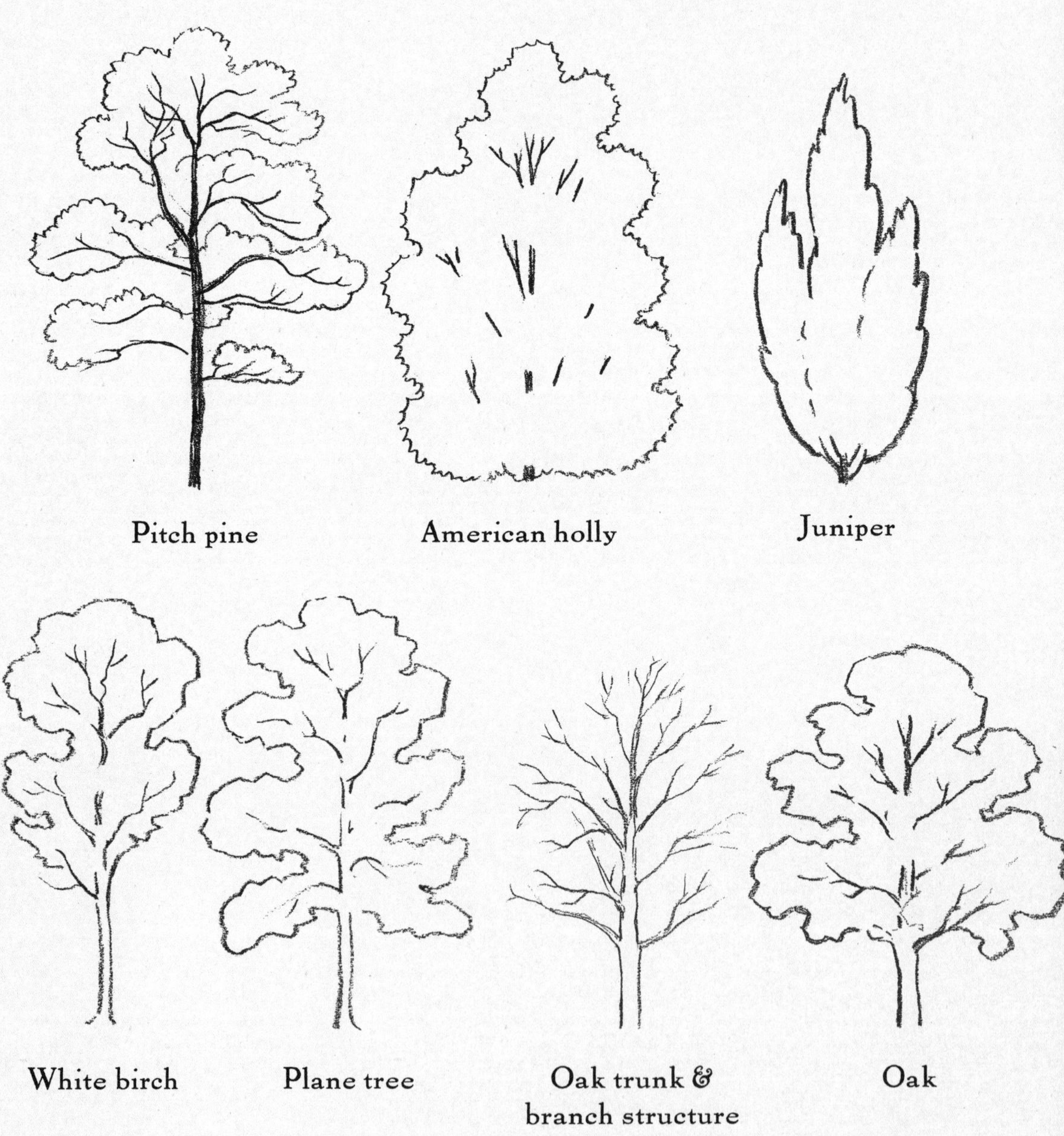

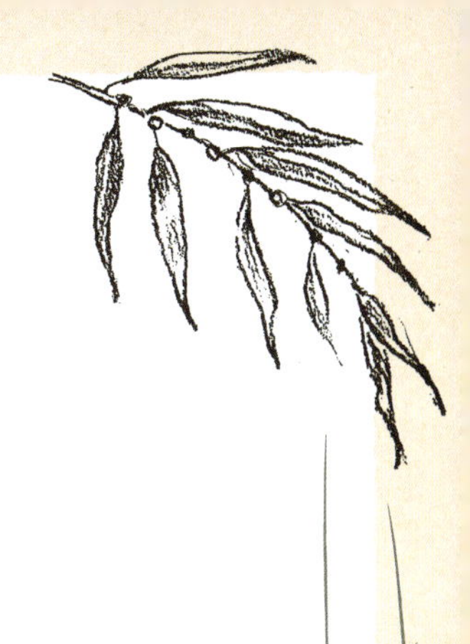

Use this page to experiment with linework. Make sure your strokes describe the weight and direction of the trunk and branches. Keep your lines loose as you block in foliage.

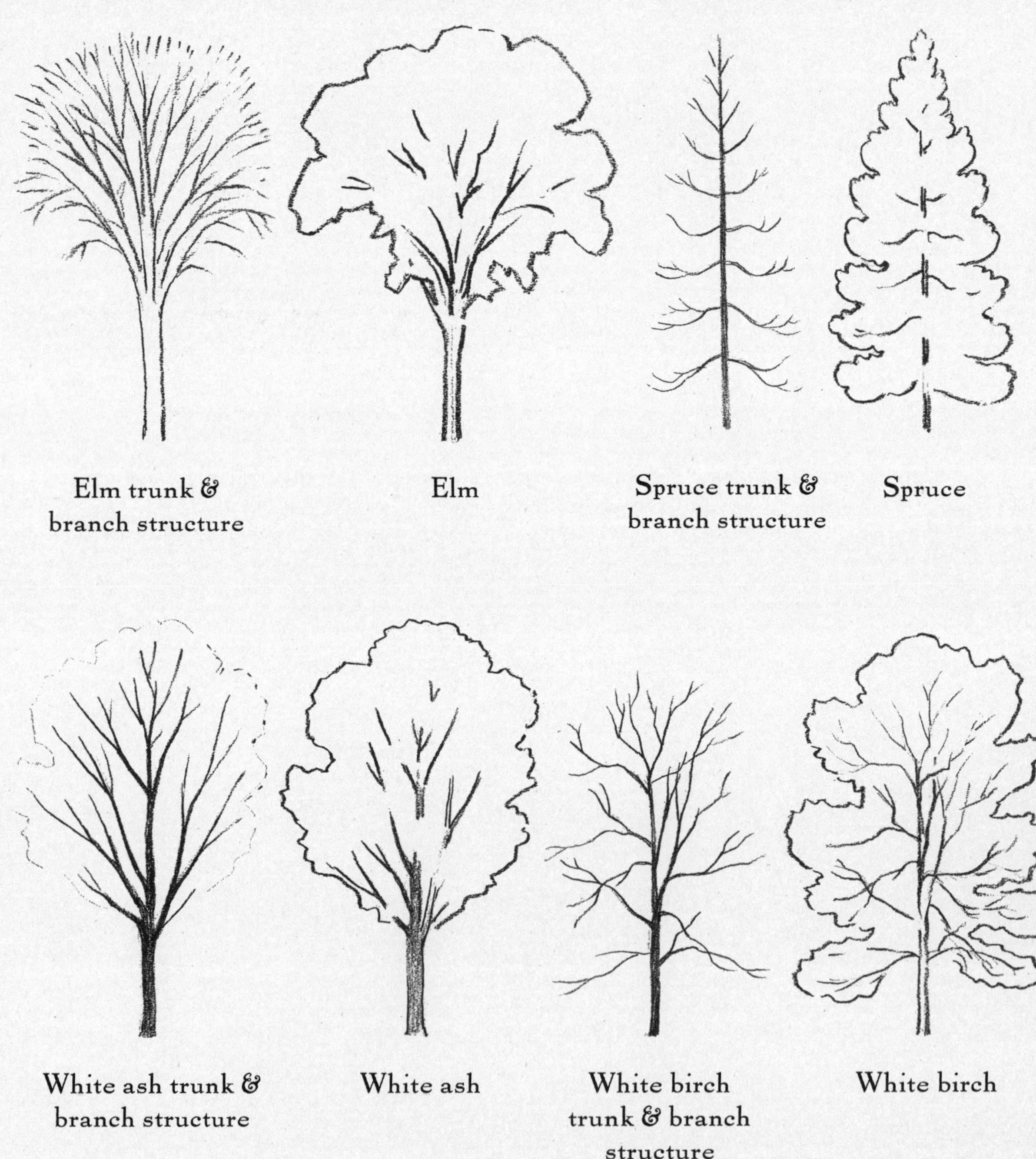

Elm trunk & branch structure

Elm

Spruce trunk & branch structure

Spruce

White ash trunk & branch structure

White ash

White birch trunk & branch structure

White birch

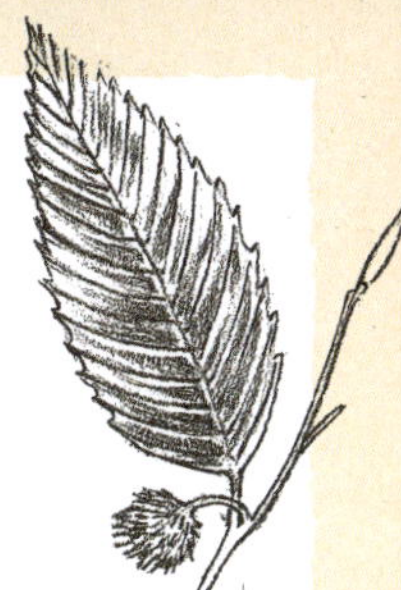

To familiarize yourself with a tree's underlying structure, create two studies: one of the tree's trunk and branches, and one of the tree's outline with foliage included.

SILHOUETTES

A student of landscape should make numerous studies of trees in silhouette. The character of the tree can be clearly brought out, and the species can be easily recognized. Studies of this kind can be made fairly quickly and are of great value for reference in later compositions.

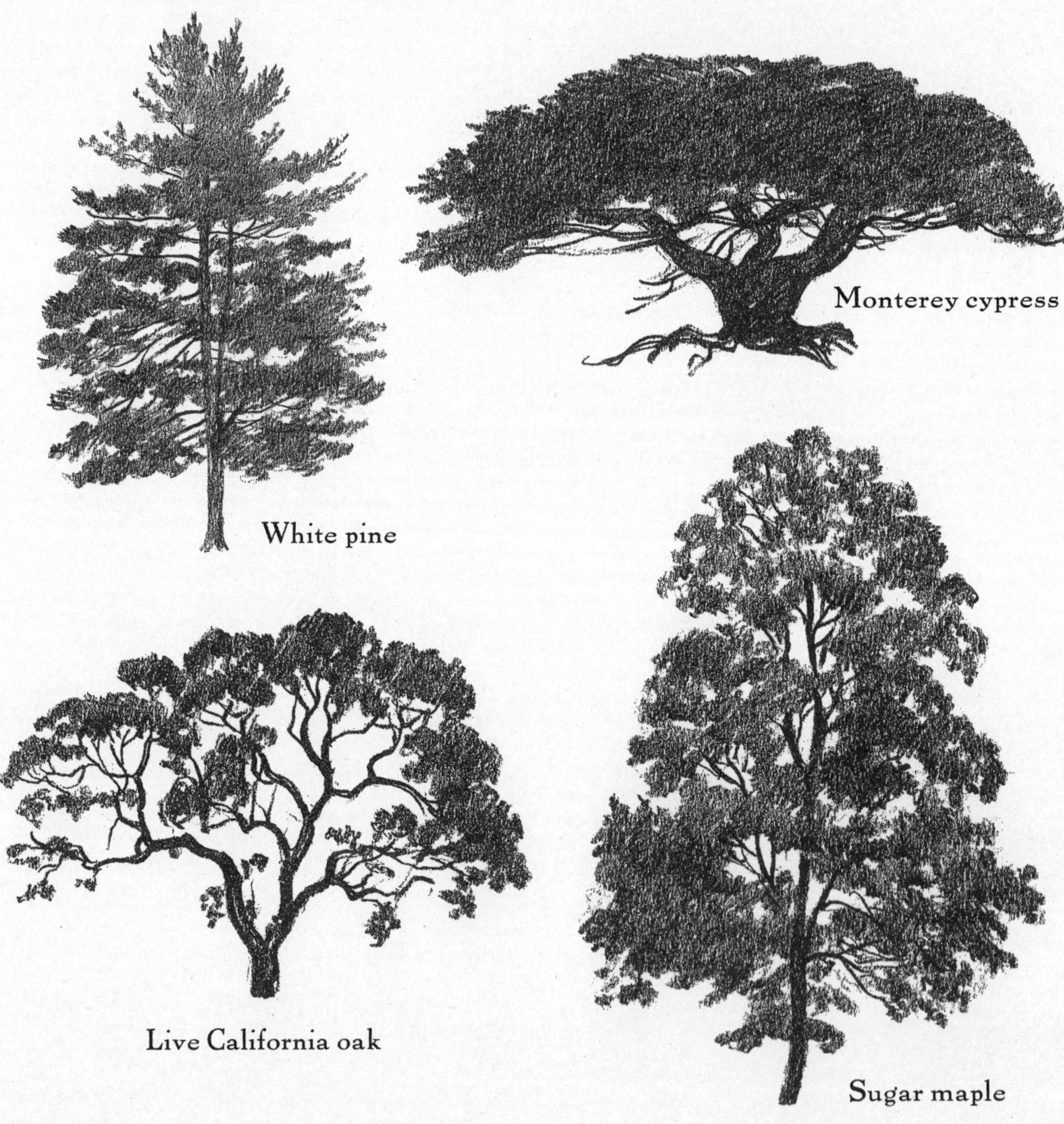

White pine

Monterey cypress

Live California oak

Sugar maple

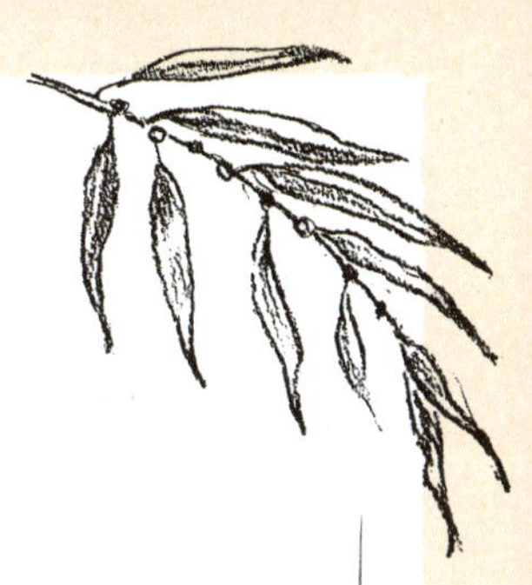

Use this space to sketch the tree silhouettes at left. Note the angle and curvature of the trunks, and block in only the basic shapes of the foliage.

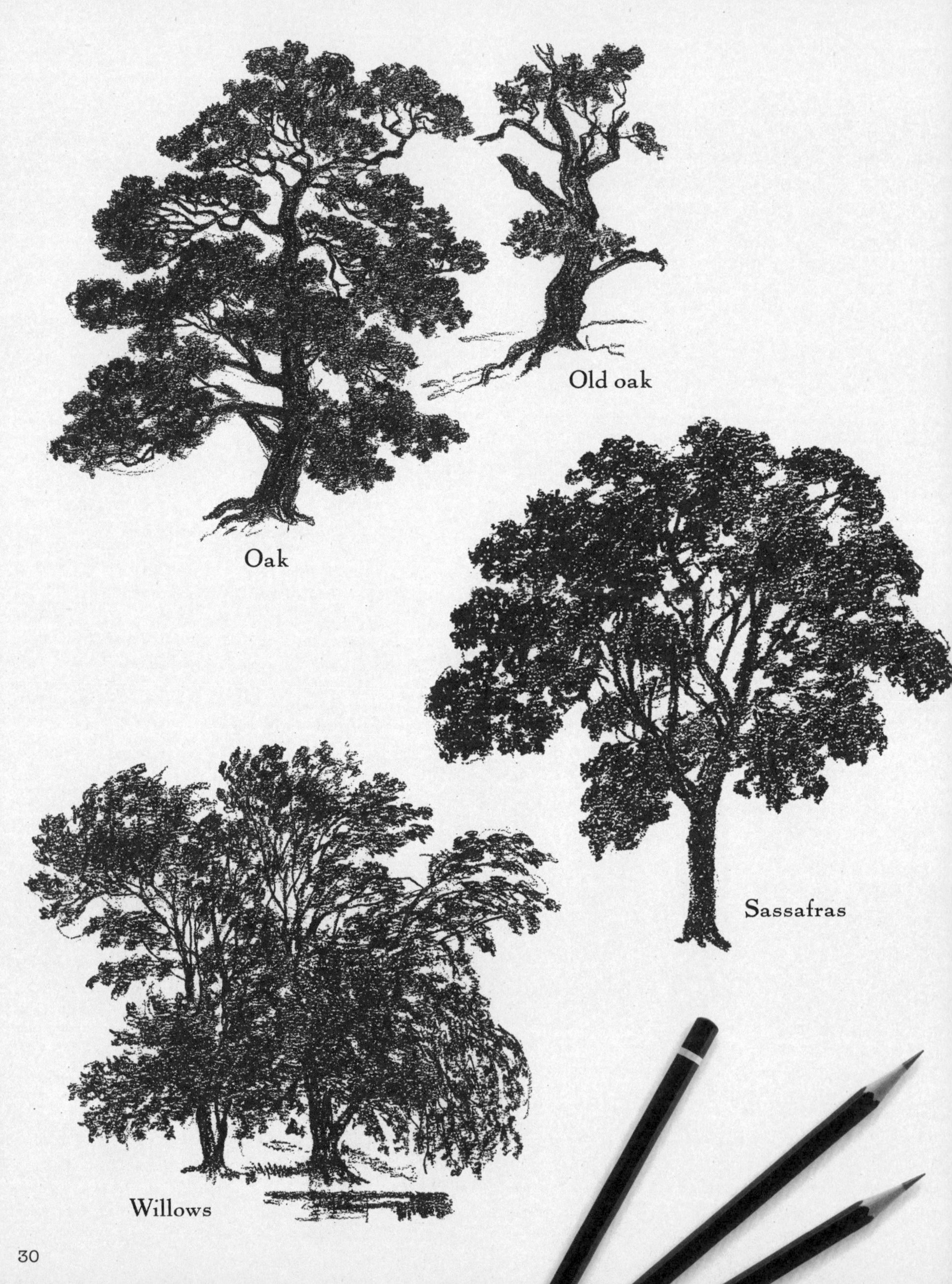
Old oak
Oak
Sassafras
Willows

Use this space to sketch the tree silhouettes at left.

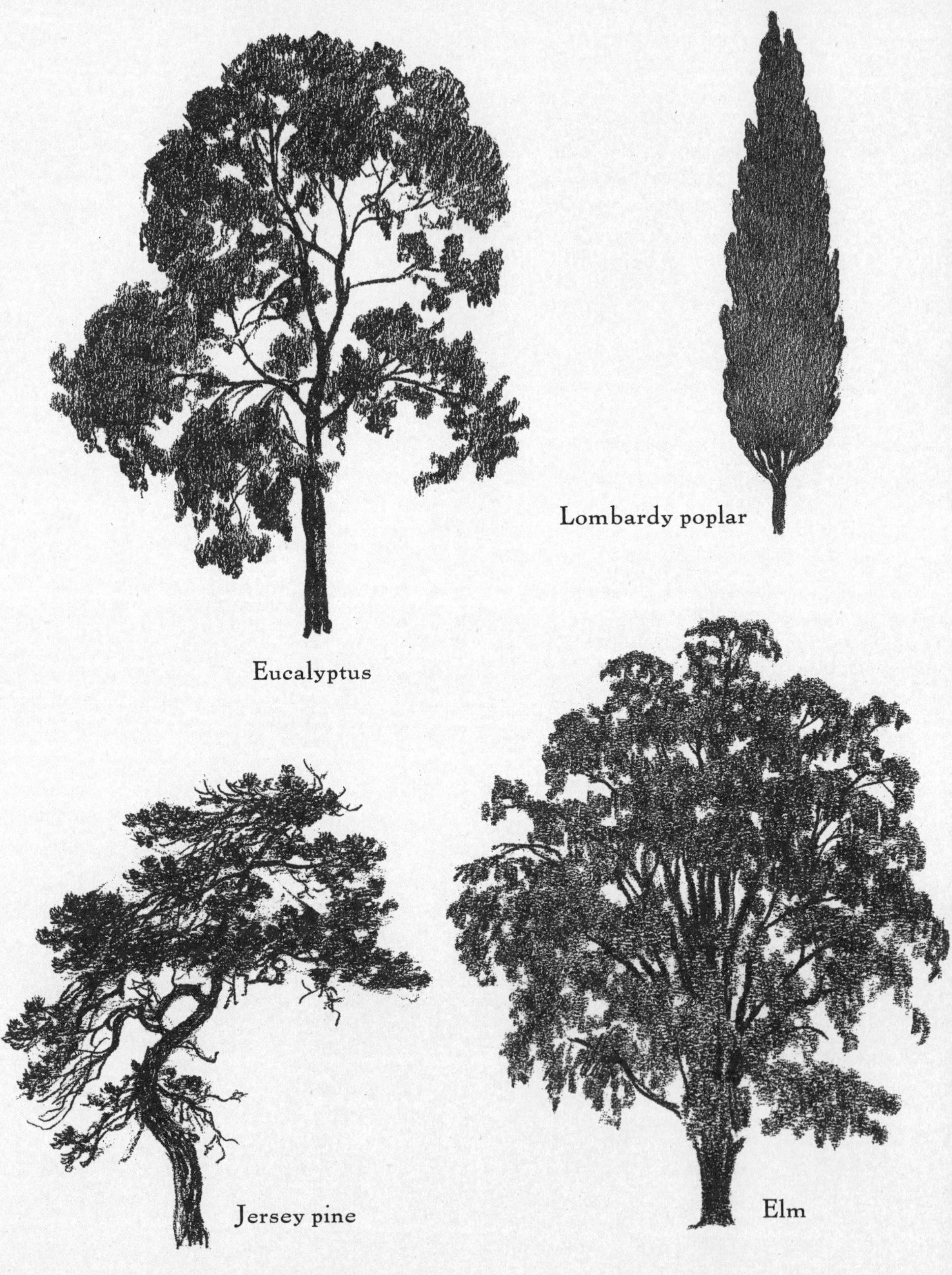
Lombardy poplar
Eucalyptus
Jersey pine
Elm

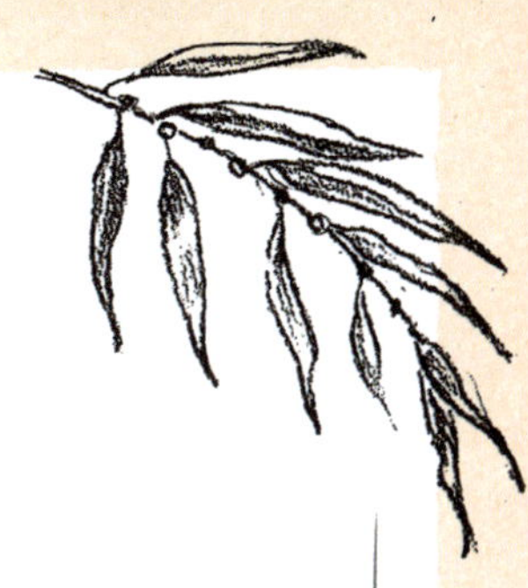

Use this space to sketch the tree silhouettes at left.

TREE STUDIES

A sketchbook is a great tool for artists to thoroughly study a subject. Use it to record notes, draw from nature, and practice your skills. The following pages feature studies of various tree species by artist Victor Perard.

Draw the masses in outline; then lighten the lines by tapping with an eraser. Go over the drawing again, treating the foliage with a more delicate touch. Begin to shade, using the shapes of shadows to group the masses of foliage.

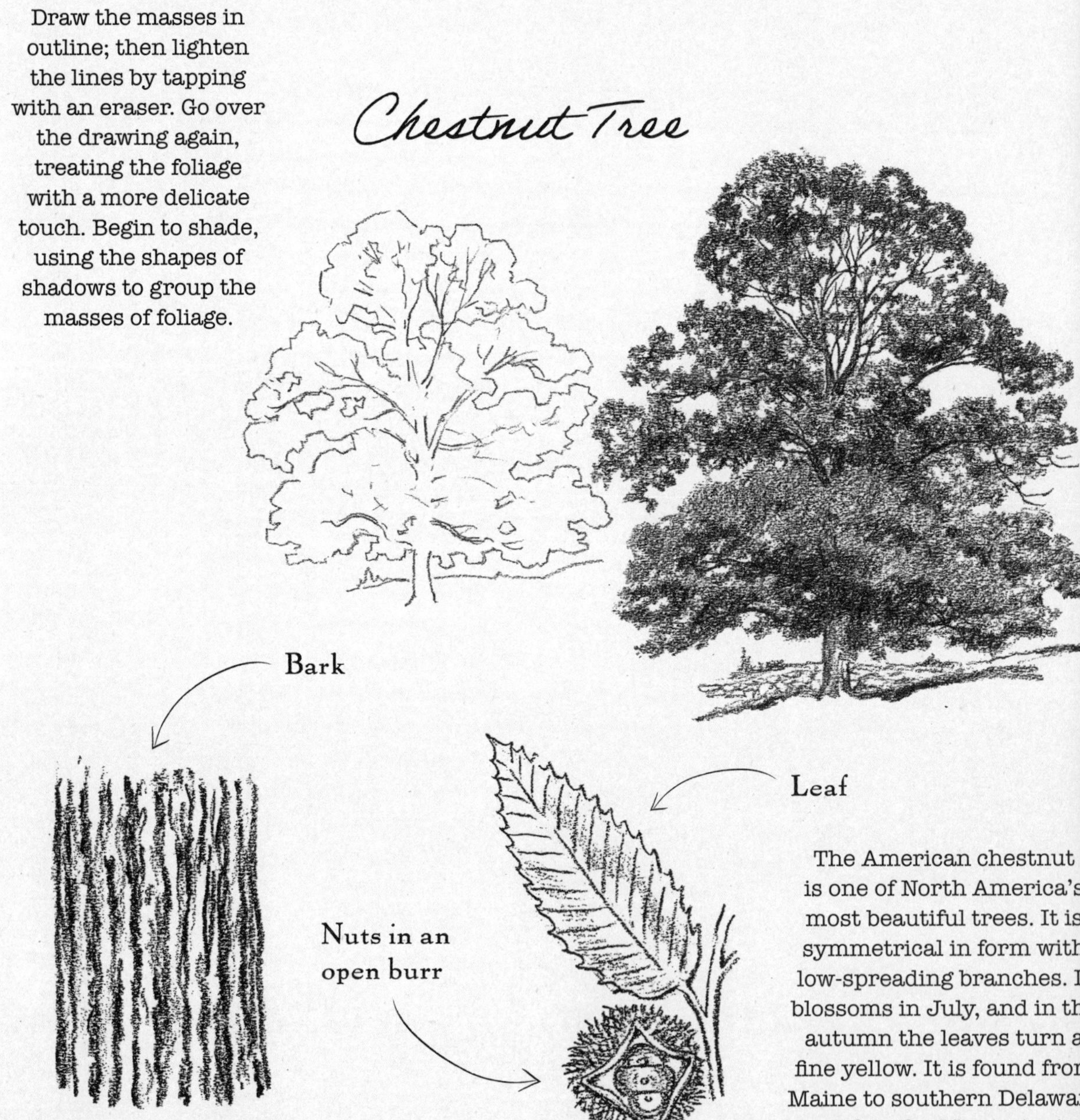

The American chestnut is one of North America's most beautiful trees. It is symmetrical in form with low-spreading branches. It blossoms in July, and in the autumn the leaves turn a fine yellow. It is found from Maine to southern Delaware and to the Mississippi.

Beech Tree

First sketch the general mass; then draw the trunk of the tree and show the character of the branches spreading from it. Finally, indicate the groups of foliage growing in masses. This makes a natural sequence.

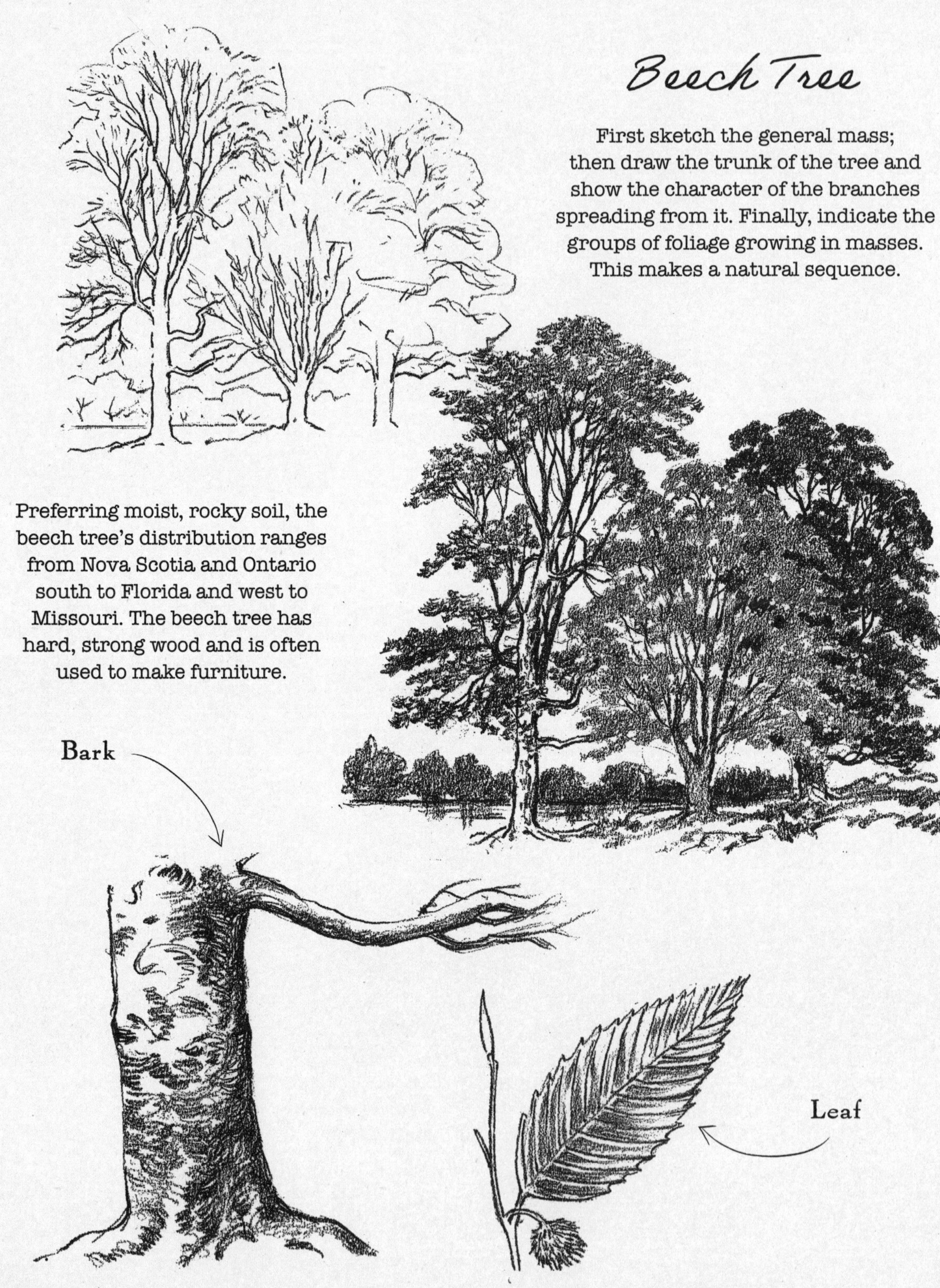

Preferring moist, rocky soil, the beech tree's distribution ranges from Nova Scotia and Ontario south to Florida and west to Missouri. The beech tree has hard, strong wood and is often used to make furniture.

Silver Maple

In this sketch, include lines full of vitality and expression, showing the struggle of a tree trying to survive after being caught in a spring freshet.

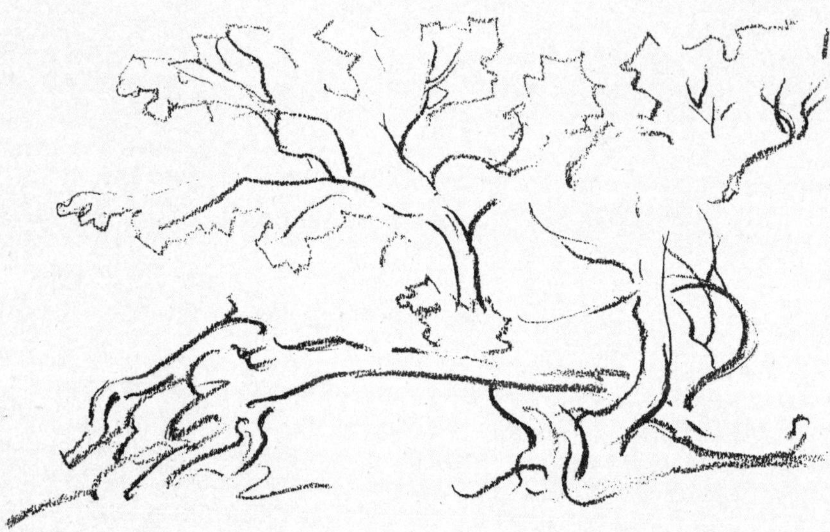

When drawing trees, try to define their type through the bark, foliage, and branching. If working outdoors in nature, make outlines of the leaves and observe all textures closely. Think of yourself as a student of the tree.

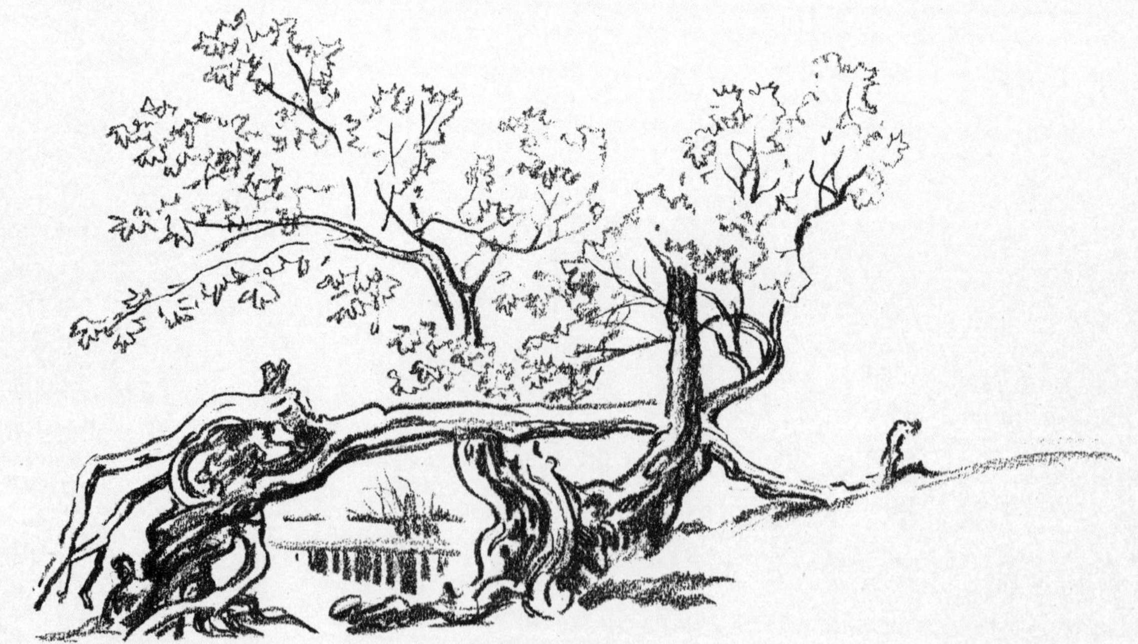

Trees of the South

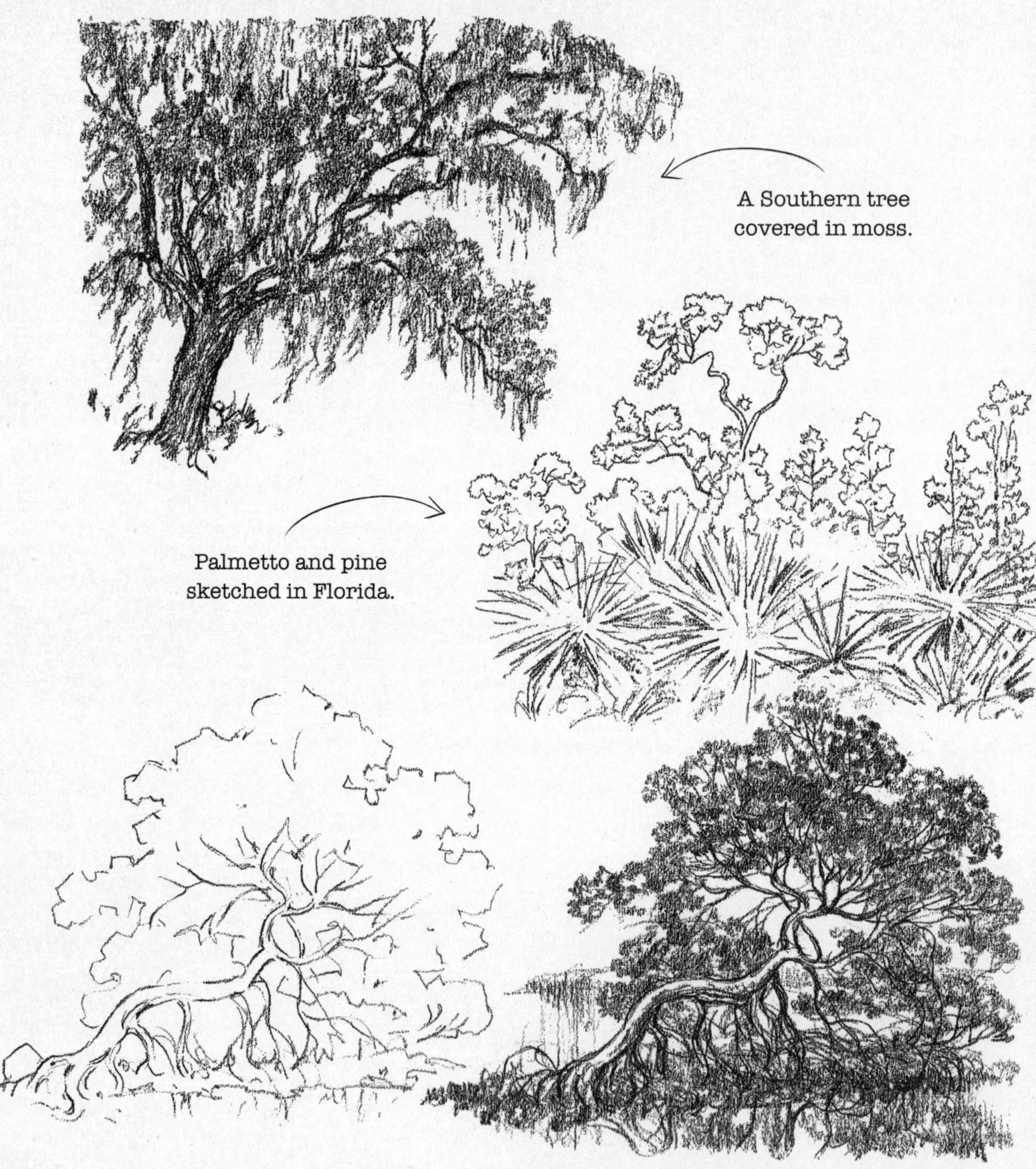

A Southern tree covered in moss.

Palmetto and pine sketched in Florida.

The mangrove is a tree that grows in swampy areas along the southern coast of the US. The branches take root and help to build the soil.

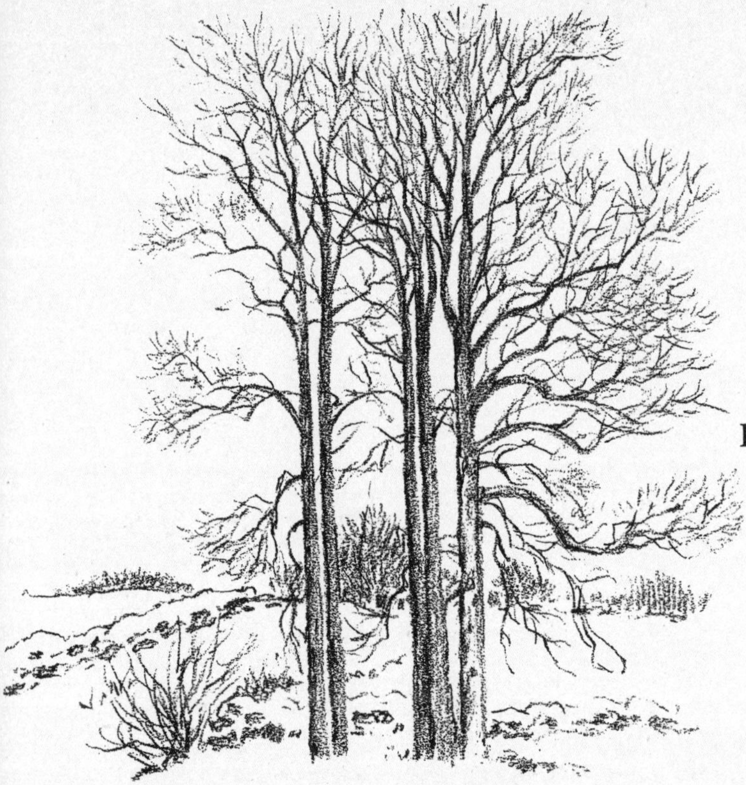

Tulip Tree

This is a large picturesque tree; it can grow up to 190 feet tall. The trunk is usually straight, and the branches are slender. The bark is deeply furrowed, and the leaves are smooth and bright yellow-green, turning to a russet brown in the fall.

Leaf

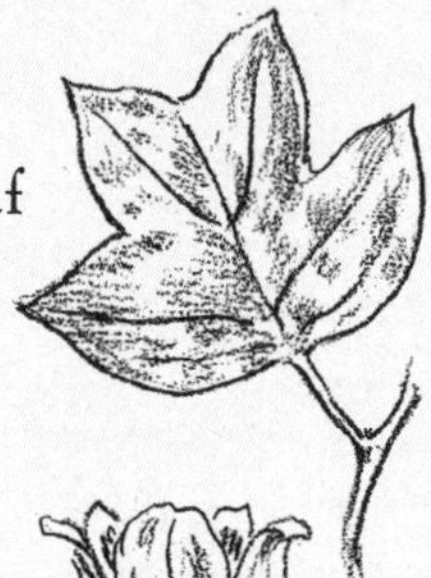

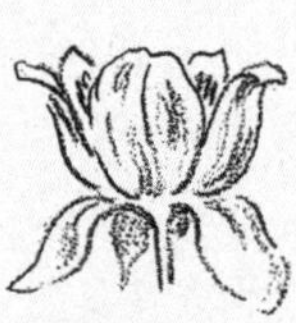

Flower

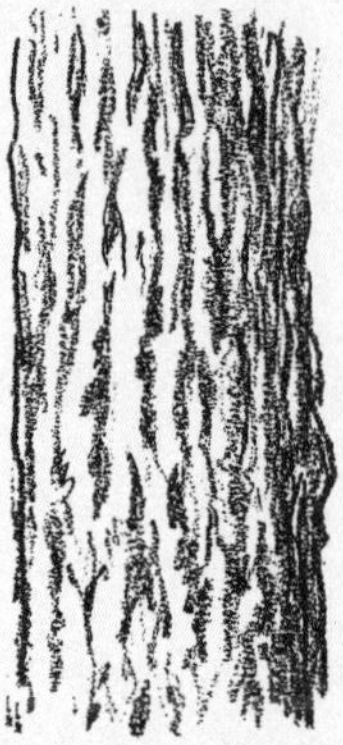

Bark

Swamp White Oak

This large tree has light brown, flaky bark. It reaches a height of 110 feet and, at times, a diameter of 8 feet. The branches are scraggly and rough with large leaves.

Bark

Leaf

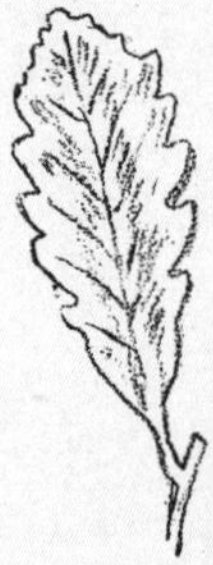

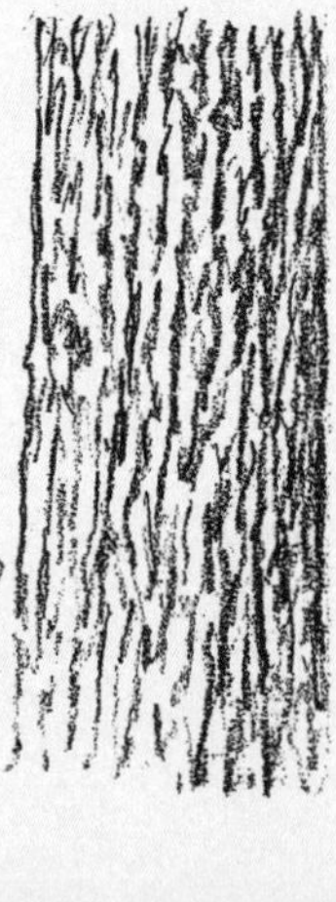

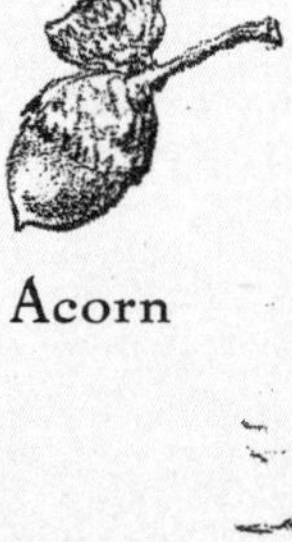

Acorn

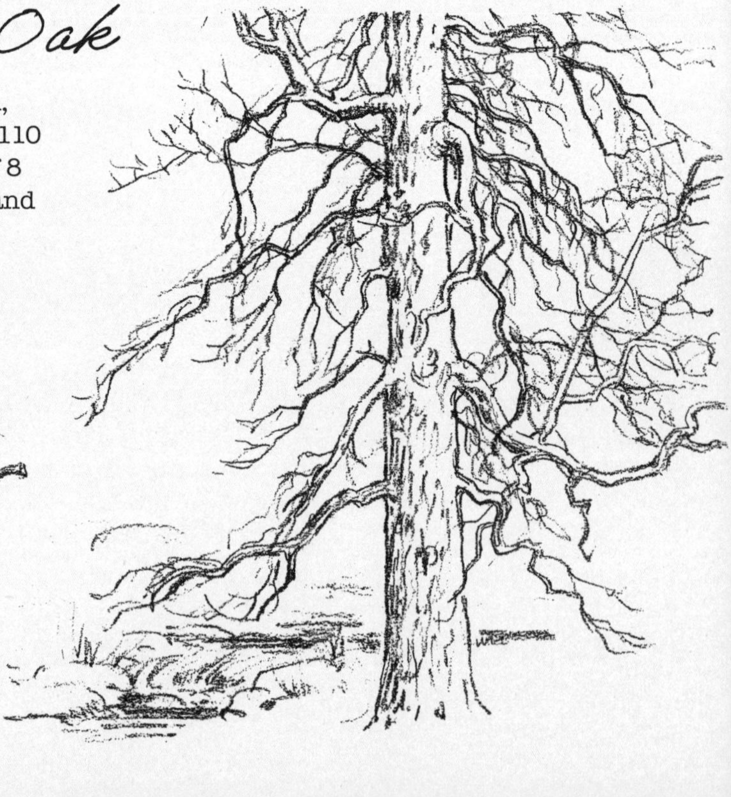

White Elm

The white elm in the US is a large tree that grows up to 110 feet high. Its trunk reaches a diameter of 1 to 8 feet. The tree divides high up into limbs that grow upward and bend gradually—and gracefully—into an umbrella form. It is found largely in New England, where it is planted on village streets as shade trees. Its distribution is north to Nova Scotia, south to Florida, and west to Texas.

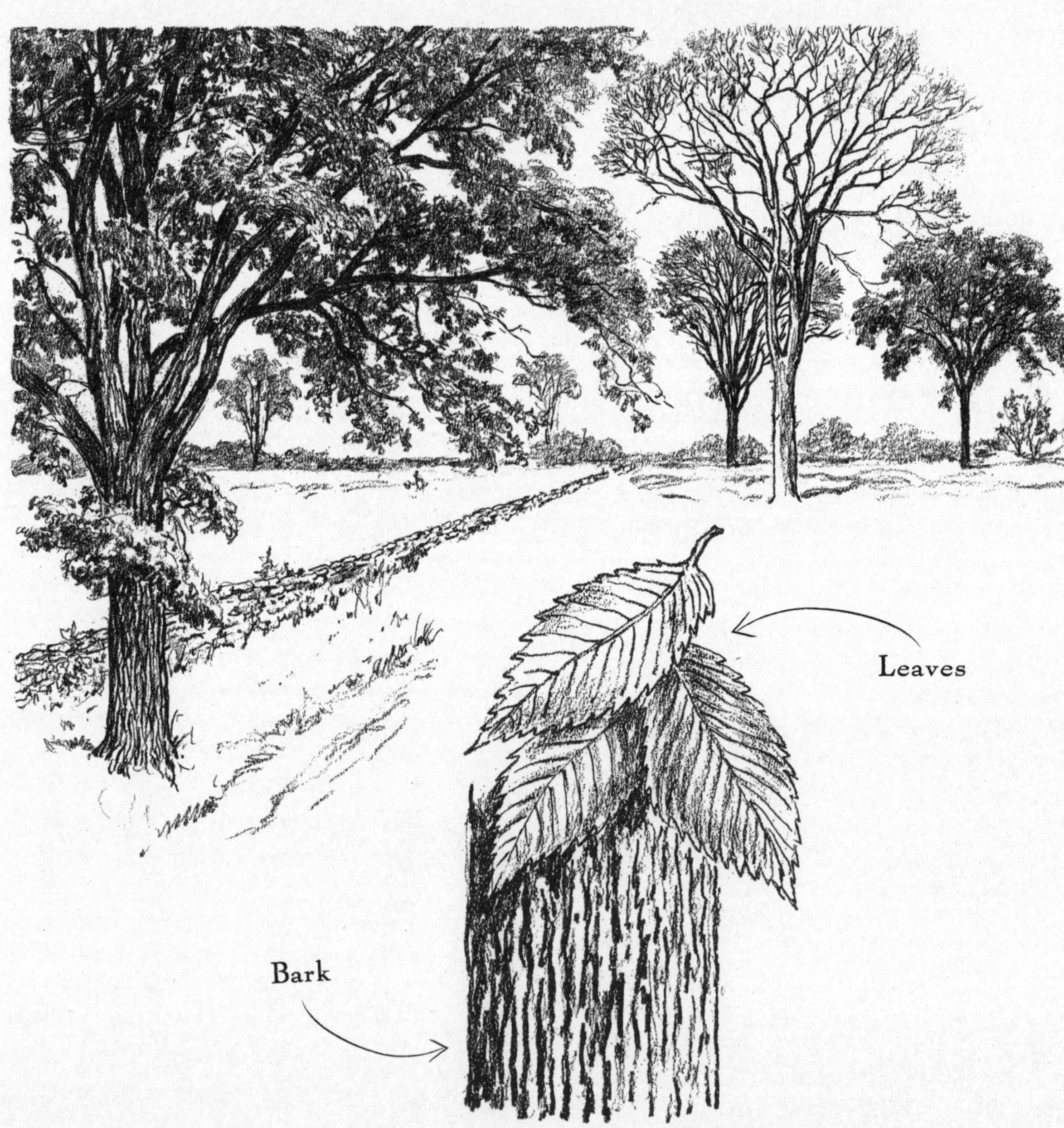

Apple Tree

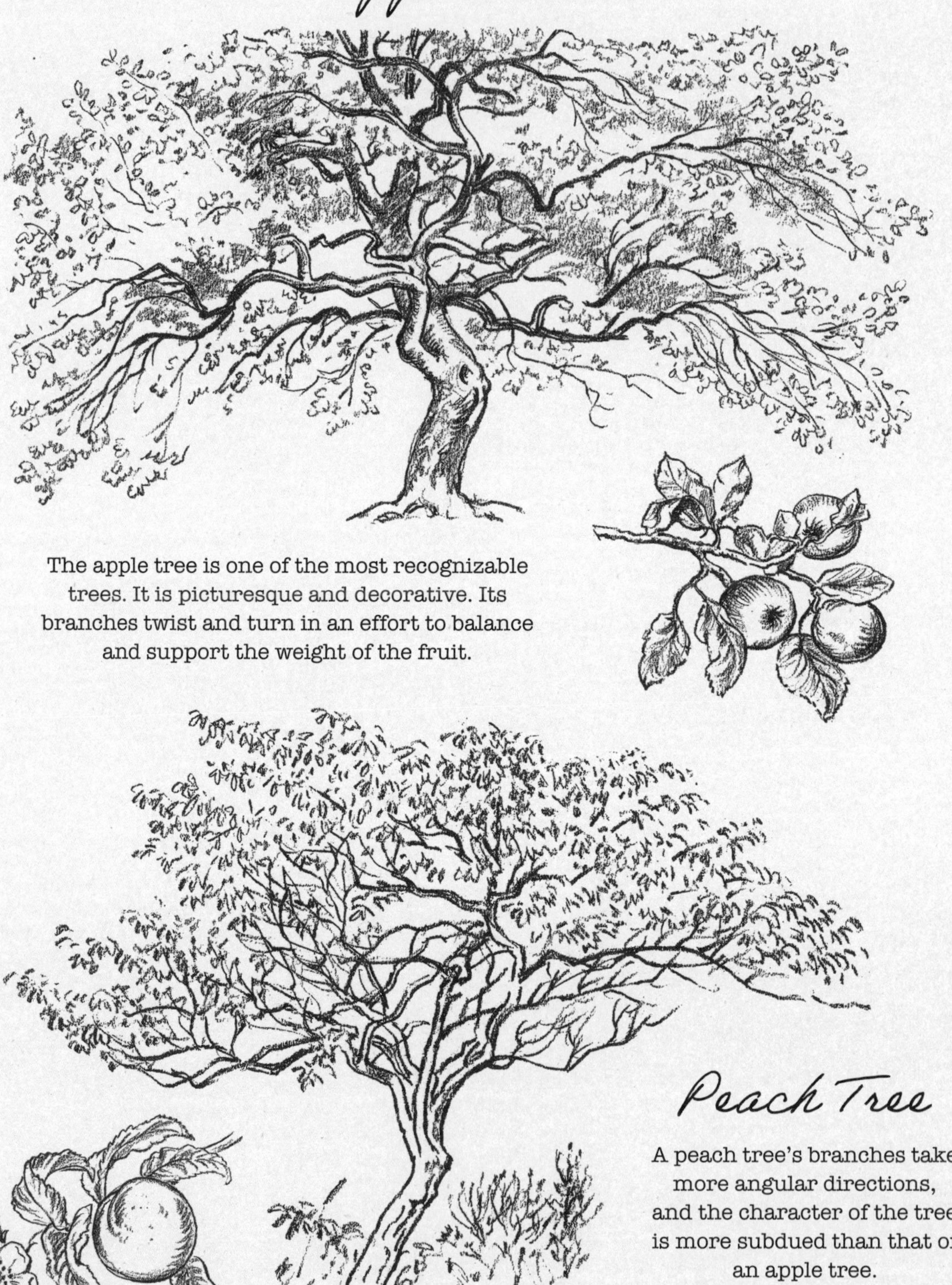

The apple tree is one of the most recognizable trees. It is picturesque and decorative. Its branches twist and turn in an effort to balance and support the weight of the fruit.

Peach Tree

A peach tree's branches take more angular directions, and the character of the tree is more subdued than that of an apple tree.

Cypress Tree

The cypress reaches 40 to 75 feet in height and becomes gnarled and flat-topped when old. Its wood is hard, heavy, durable, and fine-grained. The leaves are small and the foliage thick. In cultivation, the species thrive and make beautiful ornamental evergreens that seem to prefer windswept hillsides.

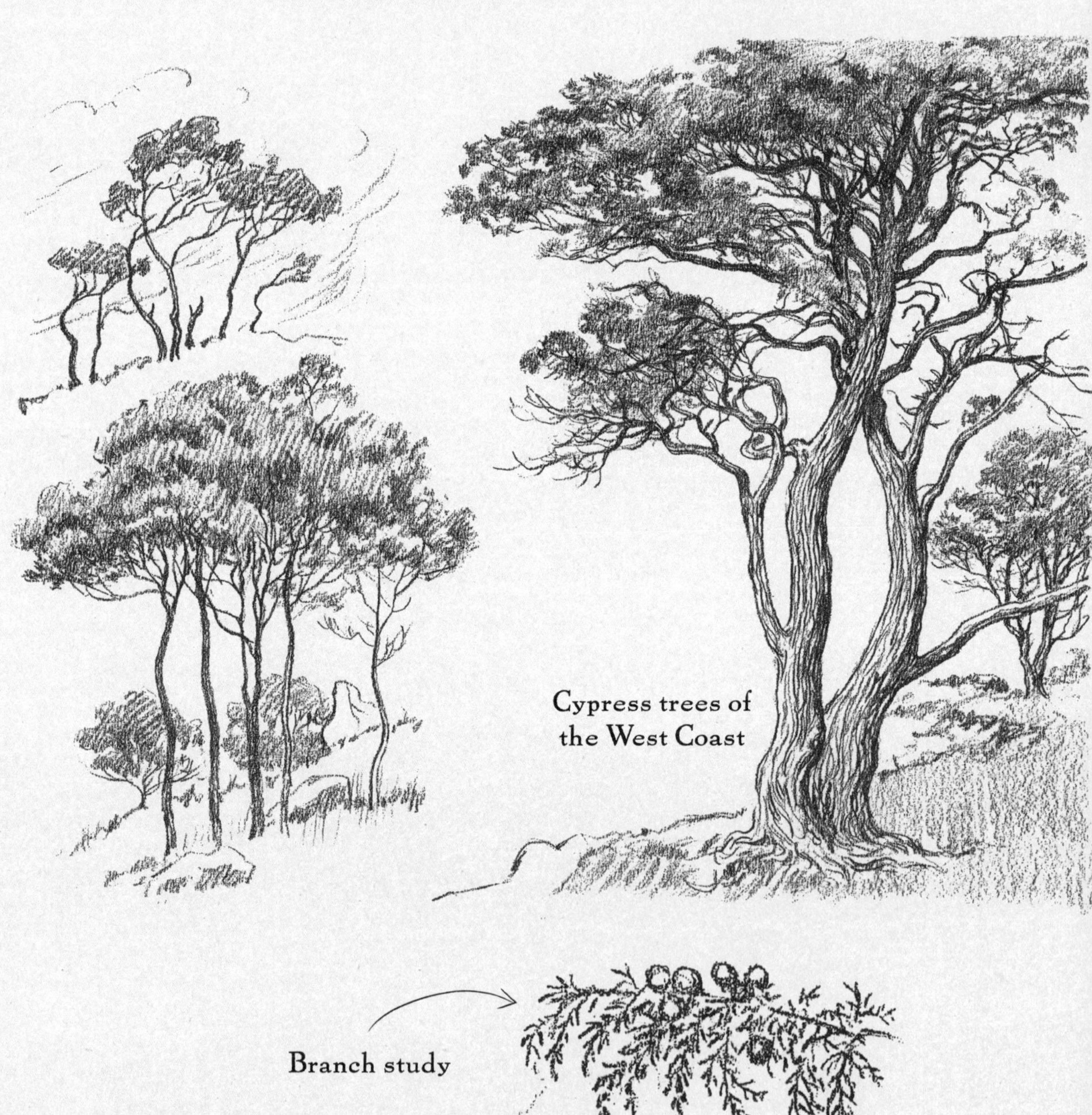

Cypress trees of the West Coast

Branch study

Norway Spruce

Preliminary lines (left) for the branches of the Norway spruce show the dripping character of the branches and needles.

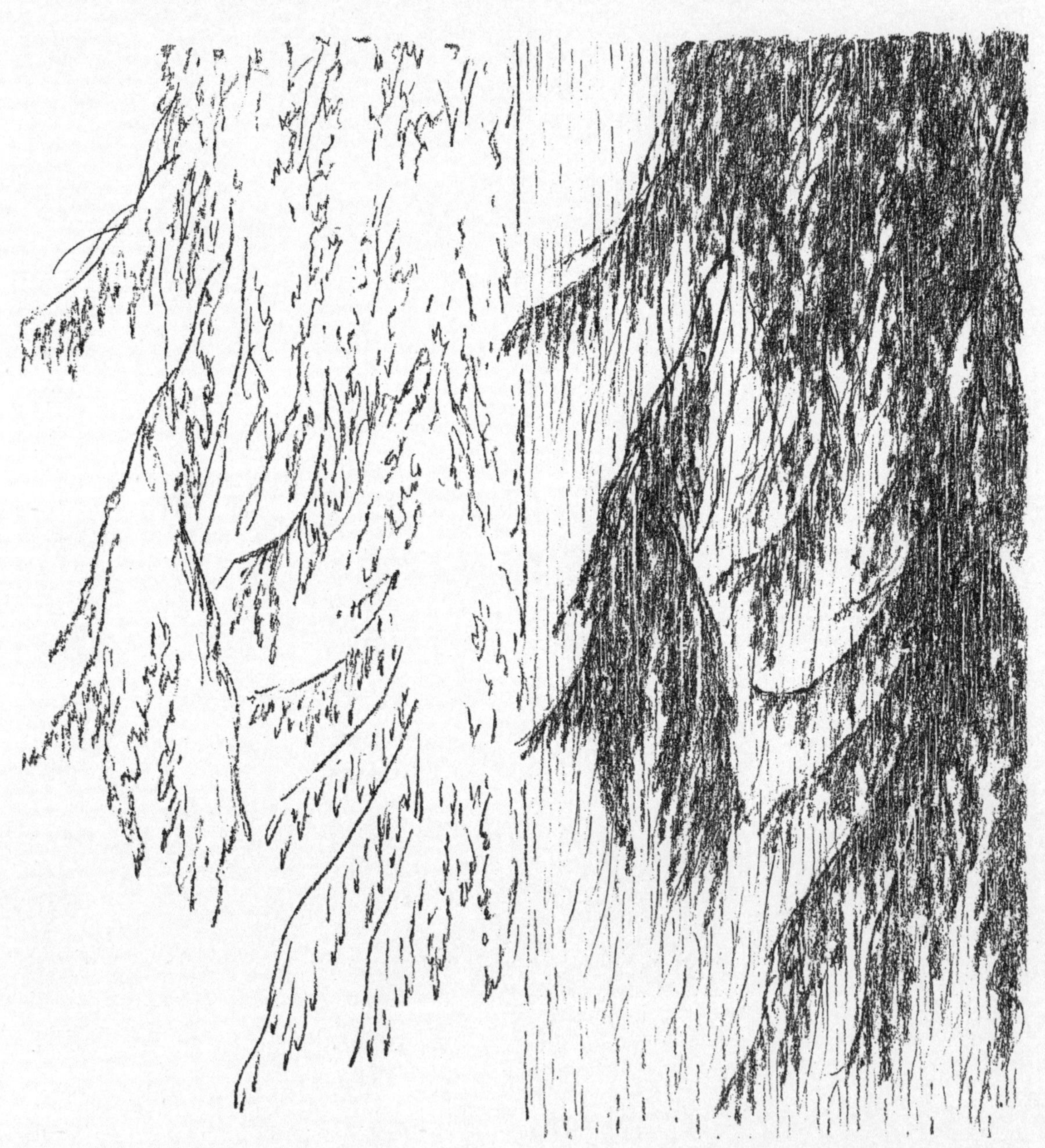

This finished study shows the Norway spruce in a rain shower.

Cacti of Arizona

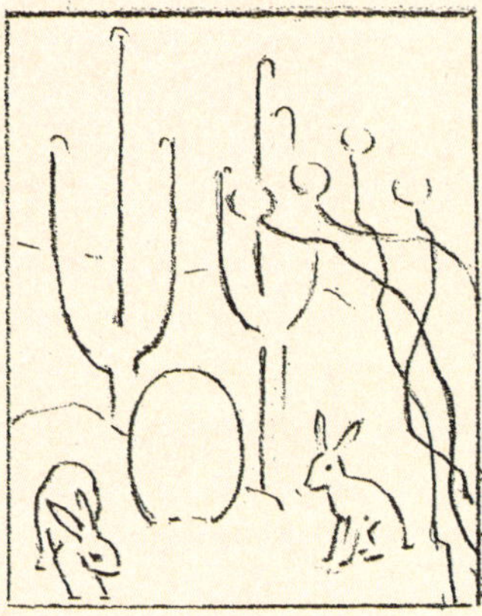

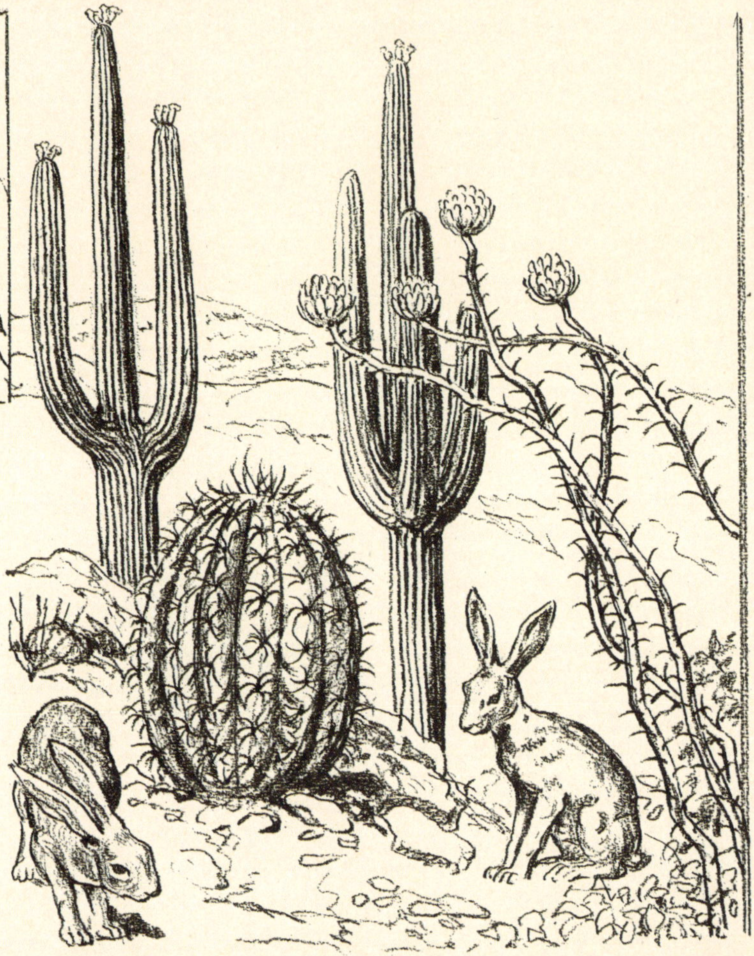

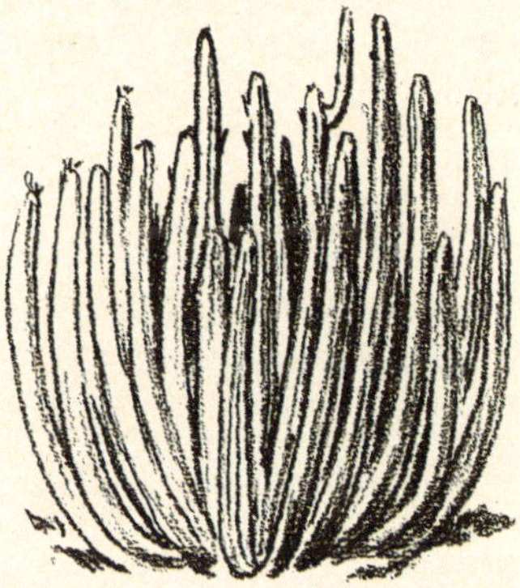

Organ cactus

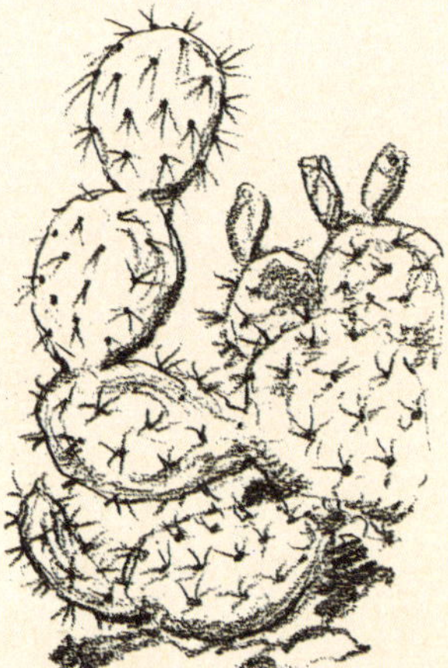

Prickly pear

Saguaro flower

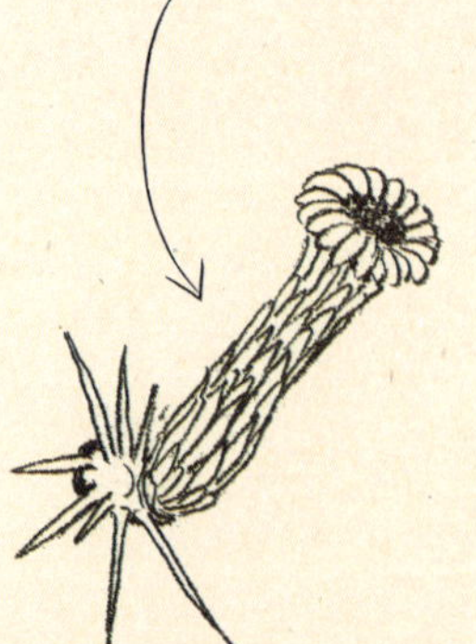

This scene features a saguaro (giant cactus), barrel cactus, jackrabbits, and more. Make different compositions using these various cactus plants. The saguaro is representative of the Arizona desert. It can grow to a height of 50 feet. Cacti are most abundant in Arizona, Texas, southeastern California, and New Mexico.

Working Quickly

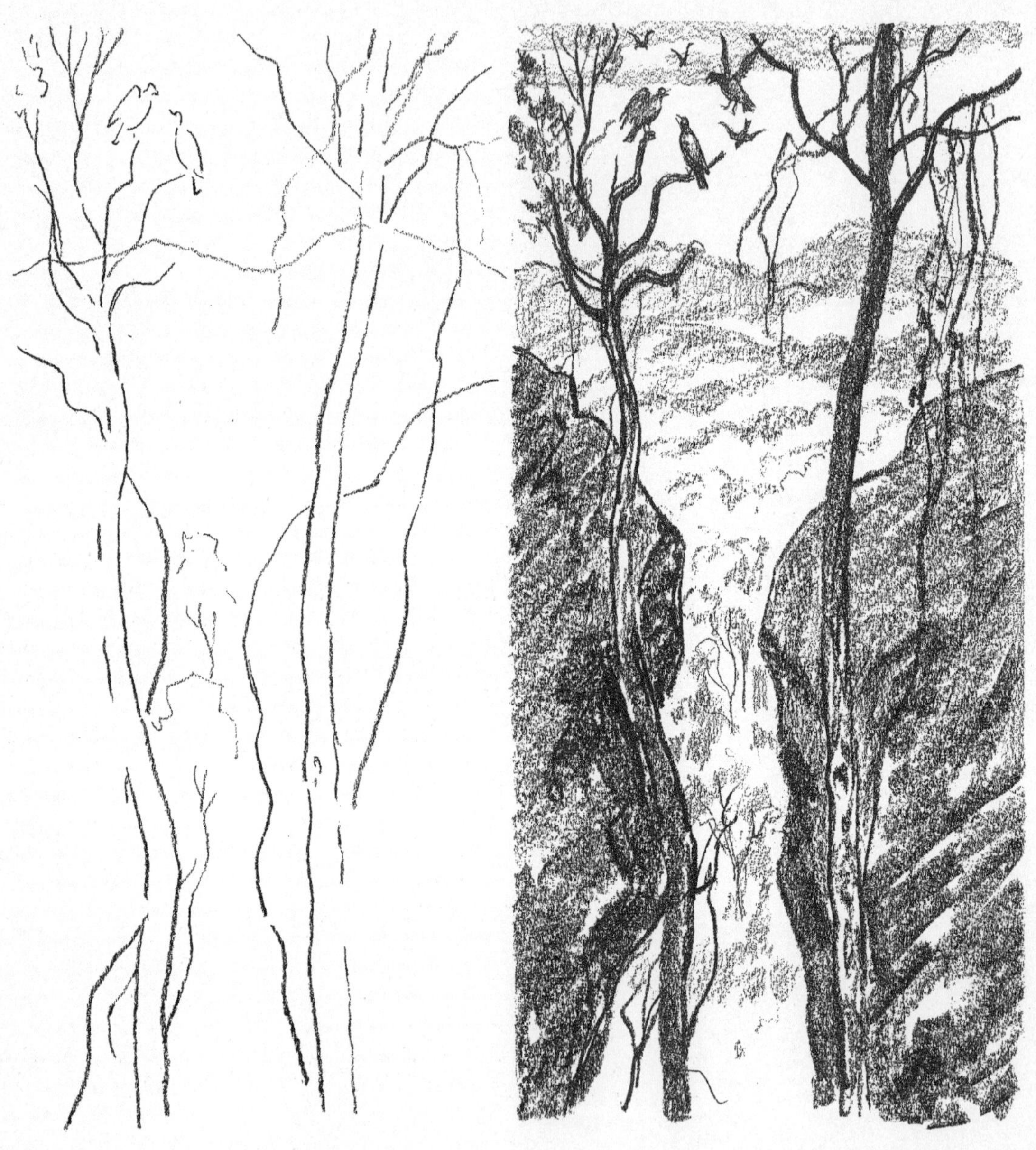

This preliminary sketch should take about 20 minutes from start to finish. After making this simple outline, wear down the side of the pencil for broad strokes. This will allow you to shade large areas quickly.

White Paper Birch

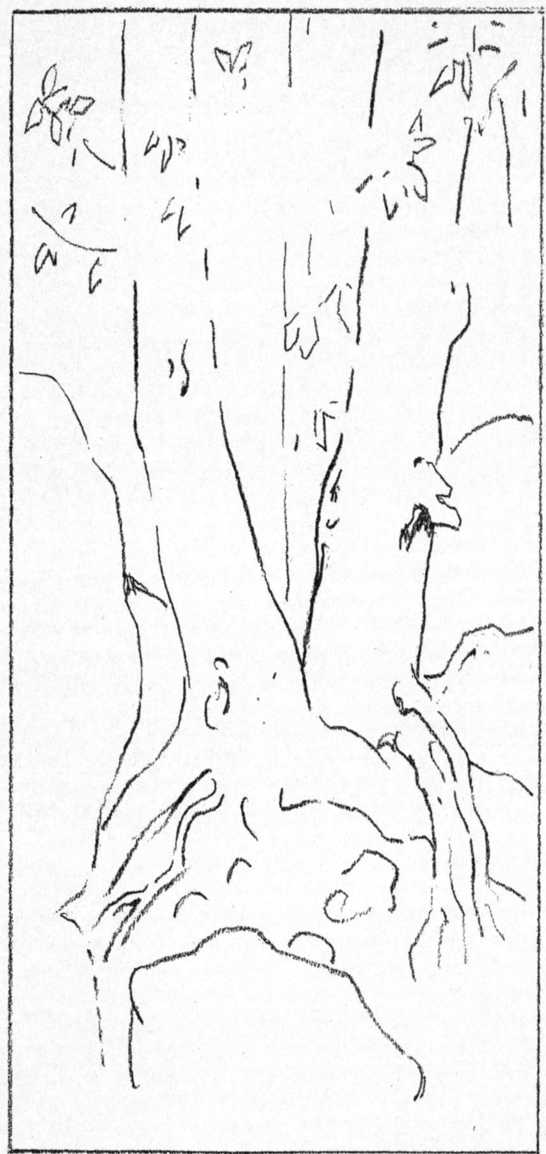

By the time the main lines of a composition are in place, the mind is usually made up as to what shading will be added.

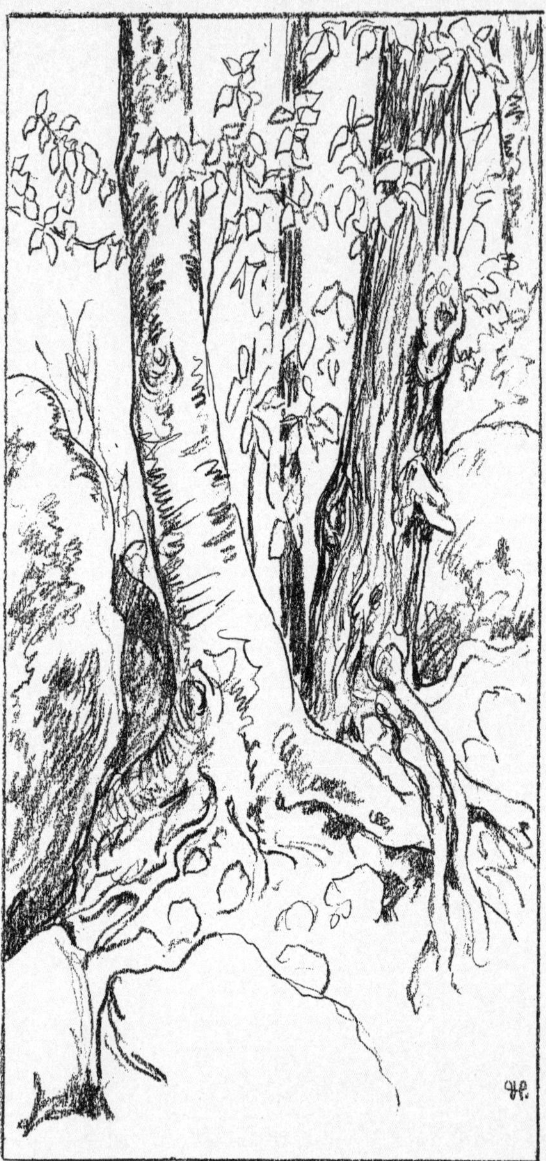

Slanting trunks and the branching, twisting roots produce an interesting sketch.

Building a Scene

Most charming nature scenes feature multiple elements—sky, trees, shrubs, buildings, and even water features. A scene like this can be overwhelming for the beginning sketch artist, but the key is to work from big to small.

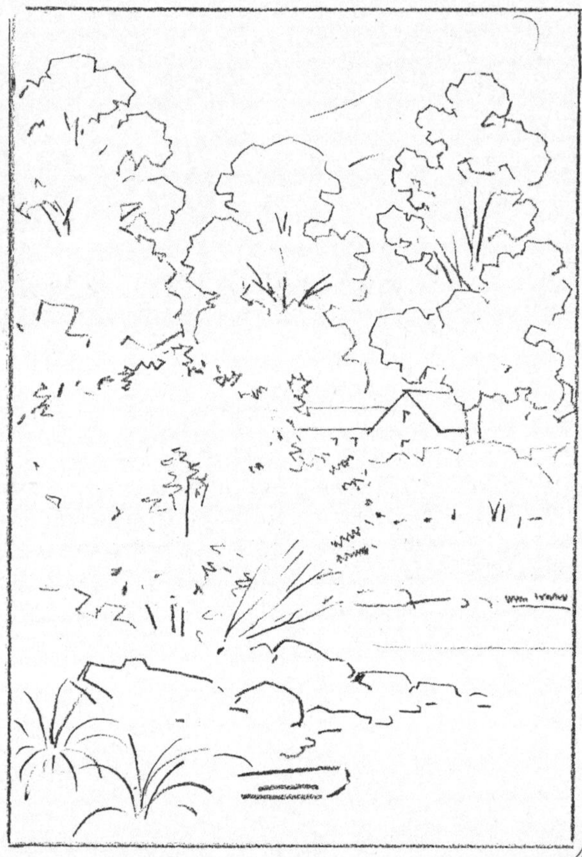

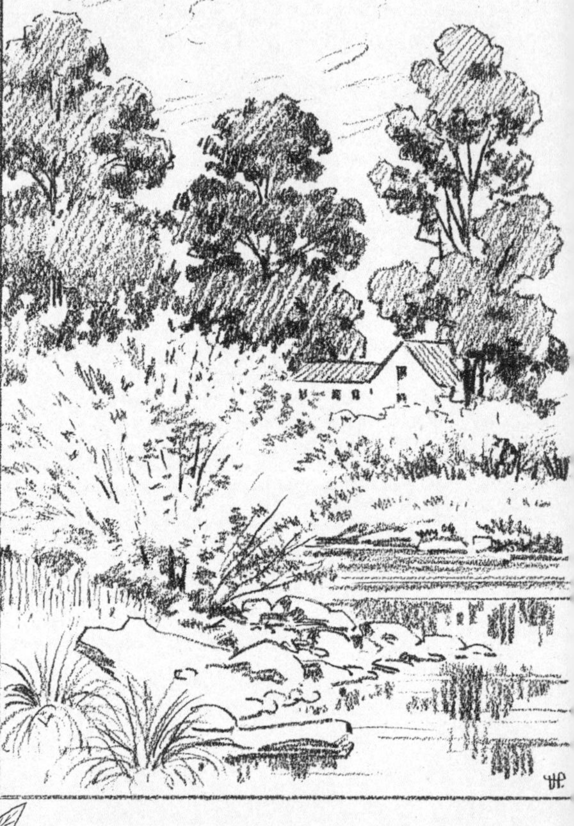

Learn to see the large forms first and the details later. A beginner, unguided, might attempt to draw the leaves on a tree first. After patient toil, the artist's efforts could be wasted if the placement needs adjustment later.

After an accurate outline is in position, a few well-placed shadows will easily complete this picture. This scene includes a poplar, a pussy willow, and a chestnut tree. Can you identify them in this sketch?

Sycamore Tree

Native to North America, the sycamore is a fast-growing tree with a sturdy trunk and a wide canopy that produces plenty of cooling shade. It is often used as a source of paper pulp and particle board.

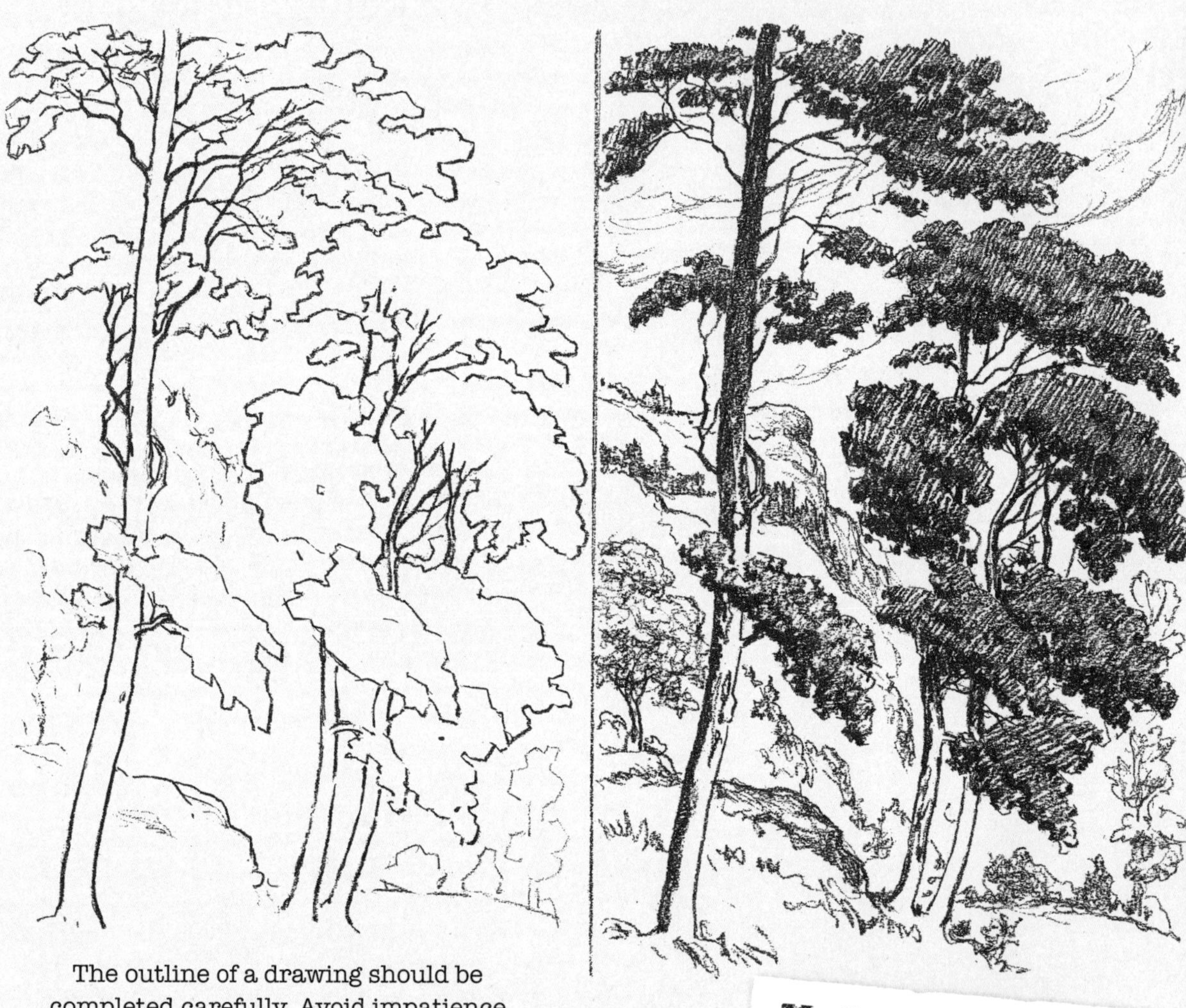

The outline of a drawing should be completed carefully. Avoid impatience at this stage of drawing.

Parallel strokes with a soft, blunt pencil are great for suggesting dense plumes of foliage.

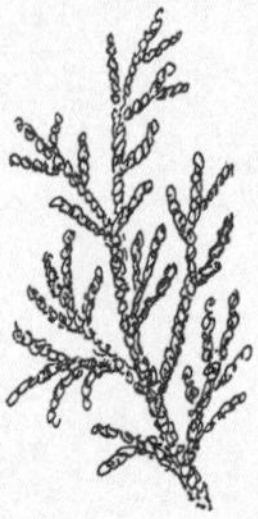

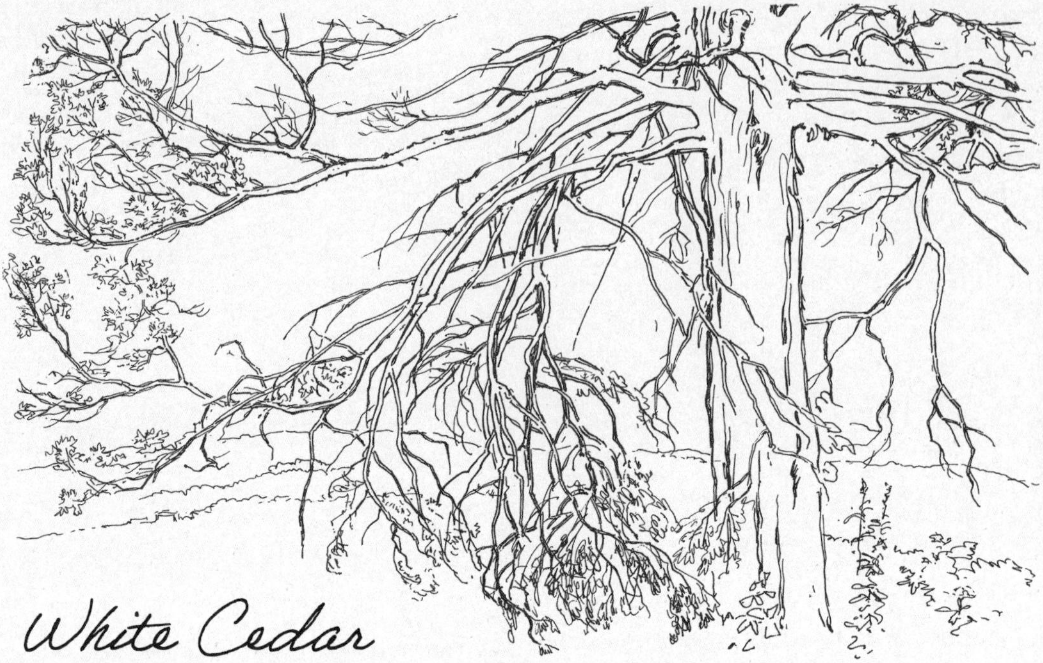

White Cedar

The white cedar is common in marshy land from Nova Scotia to Florida and west to the Mississippi. The wood is light brown in color and slightly fragrant. Its branches form interesting and decorative patterns.

This fountain pen sketch of a valley uses very little shading, with the emphasis being placed on the outline. Studies of this kind make useful references for future use.

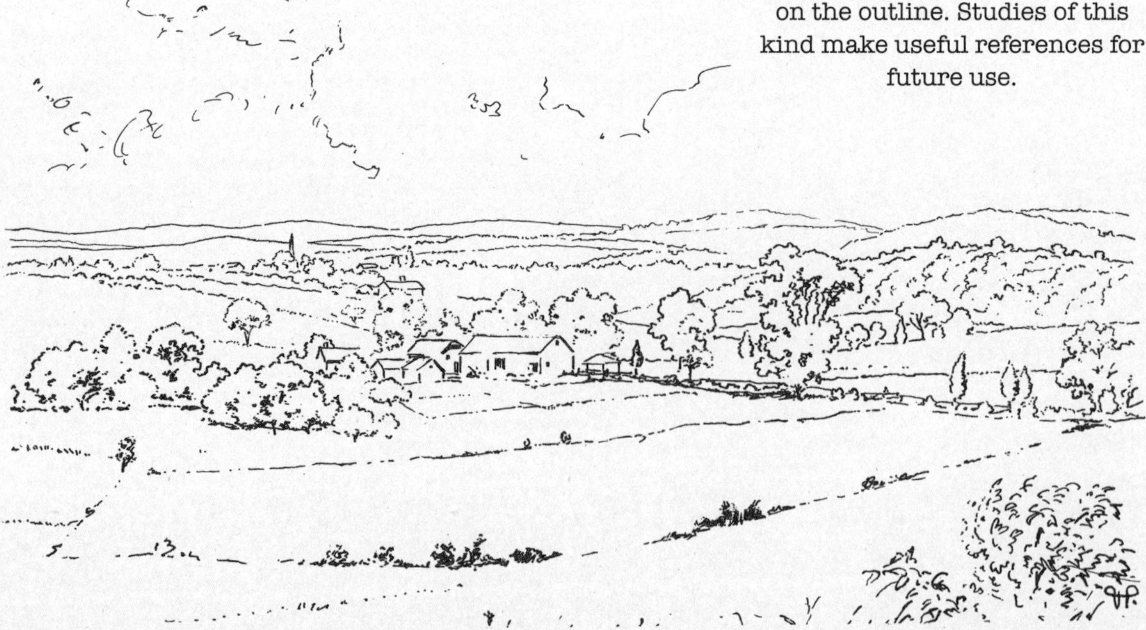

Studies in Snow

Snowy scenes are inherently rich in contrast. Use soft pencils to boldly sketch your winter scenes, leaving the ground simple and white while focusing any detail work on other elements, such as trees, water features, and buildings.

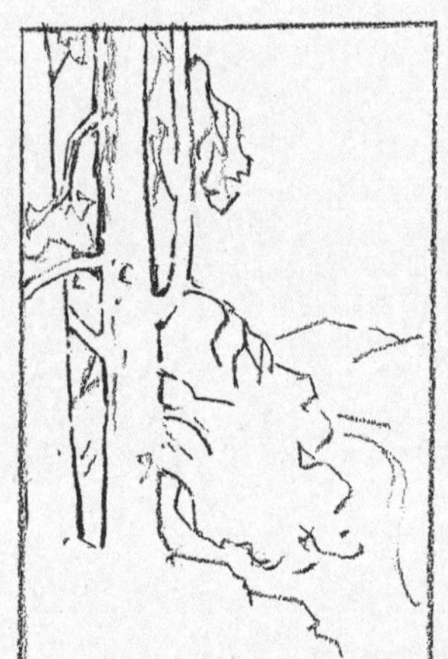

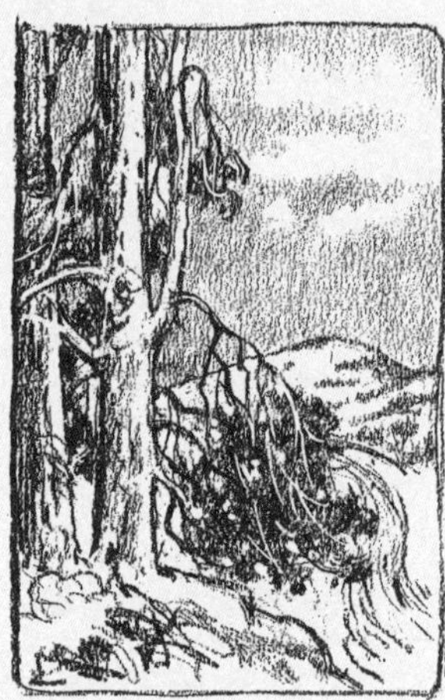

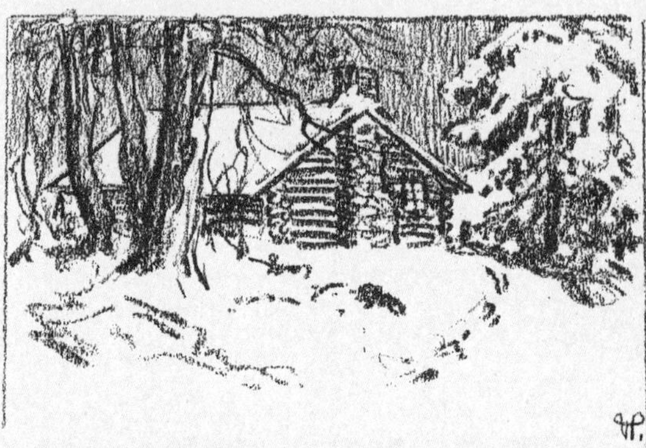

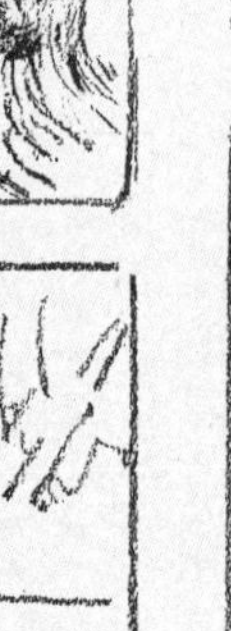

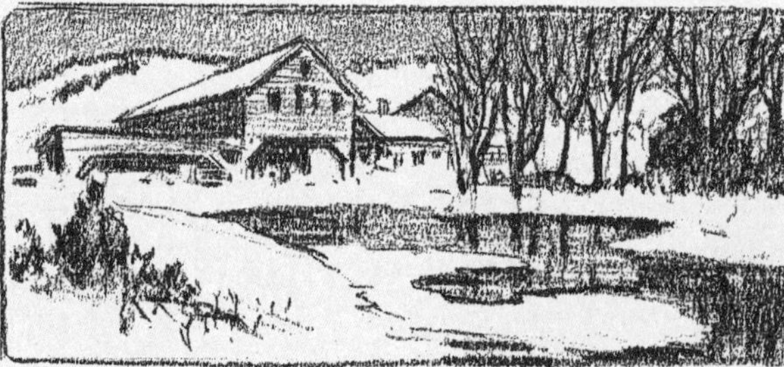

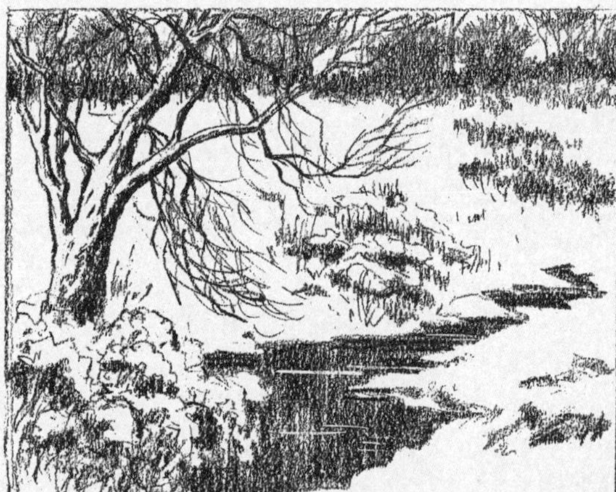

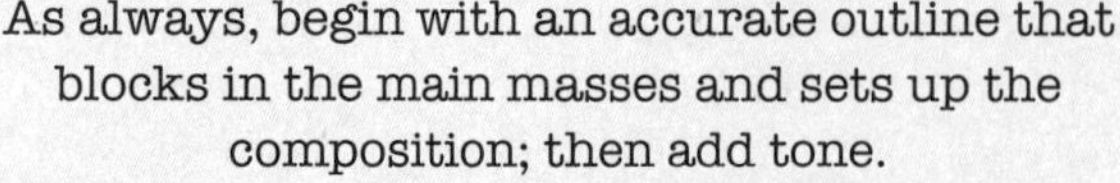

As always, begin with an accurate outline that blocks in the main masses and sets up the composition; then add tone.

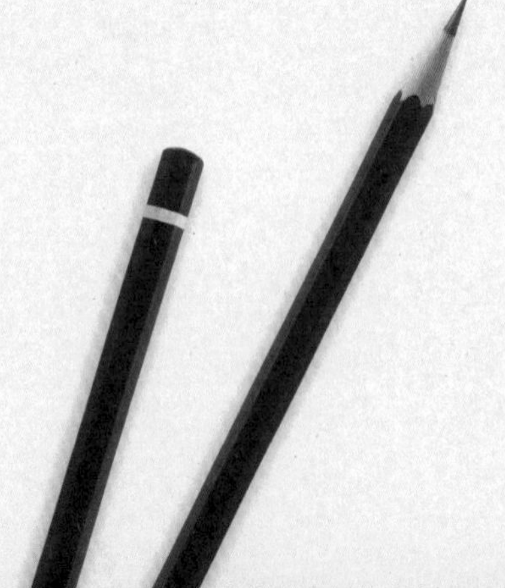

Maintaining Simplicity

This layered landscape features simple patterns using horizontal lines and a few flat tones.

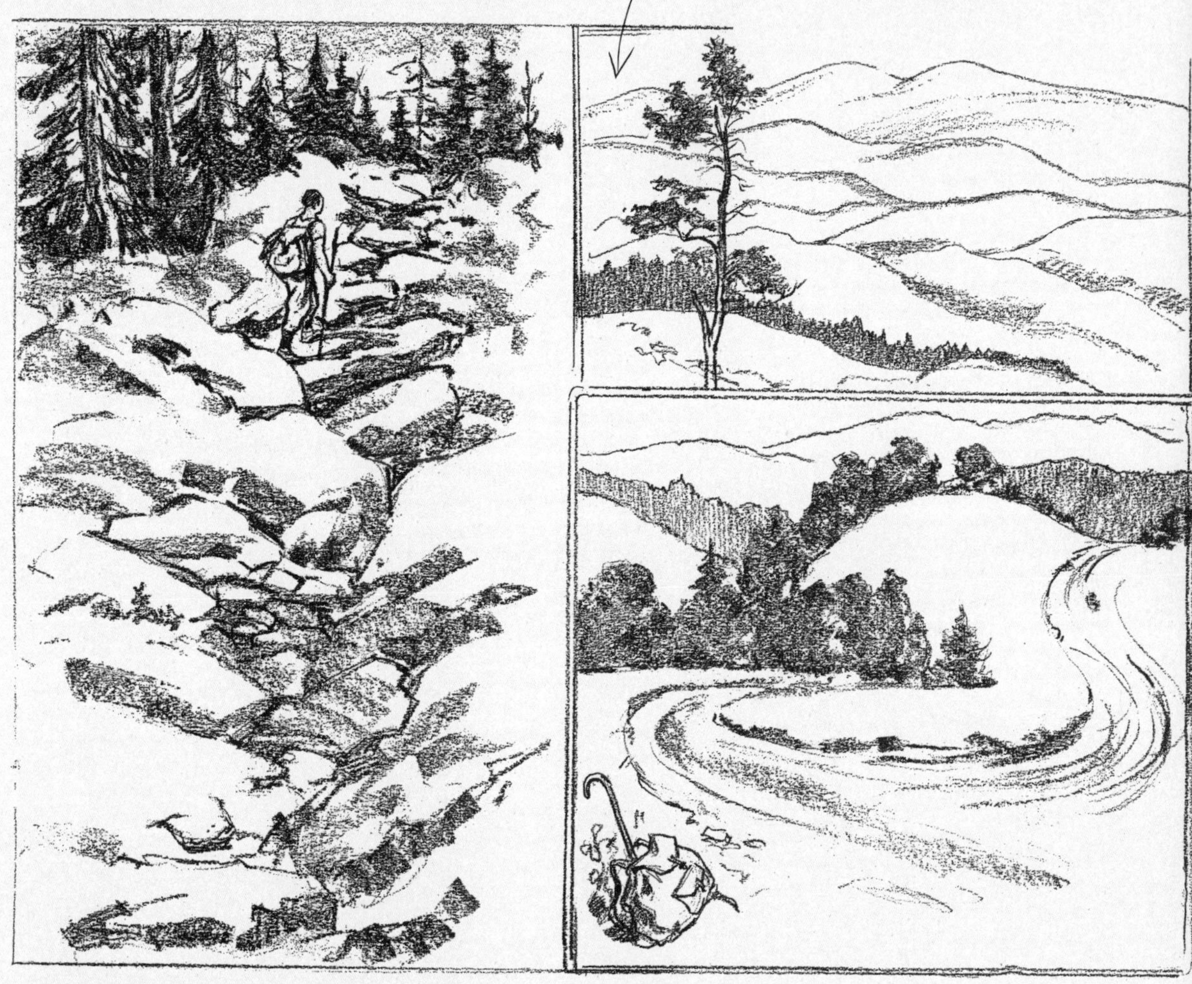

The vertical format of this sketch emphasizes the uphill nature of this hike. The rocky ravine is shaded with wide strokes using the broad side of the pencil tip. This is a simple way to build shadows and depth quickly.

This road takes an interesting turn. If too much detail is added, the design may get lost.

More Nature Sketches

Practice your skills by copying this sketch, focusing on the details of the trees, plants, and foliage below.

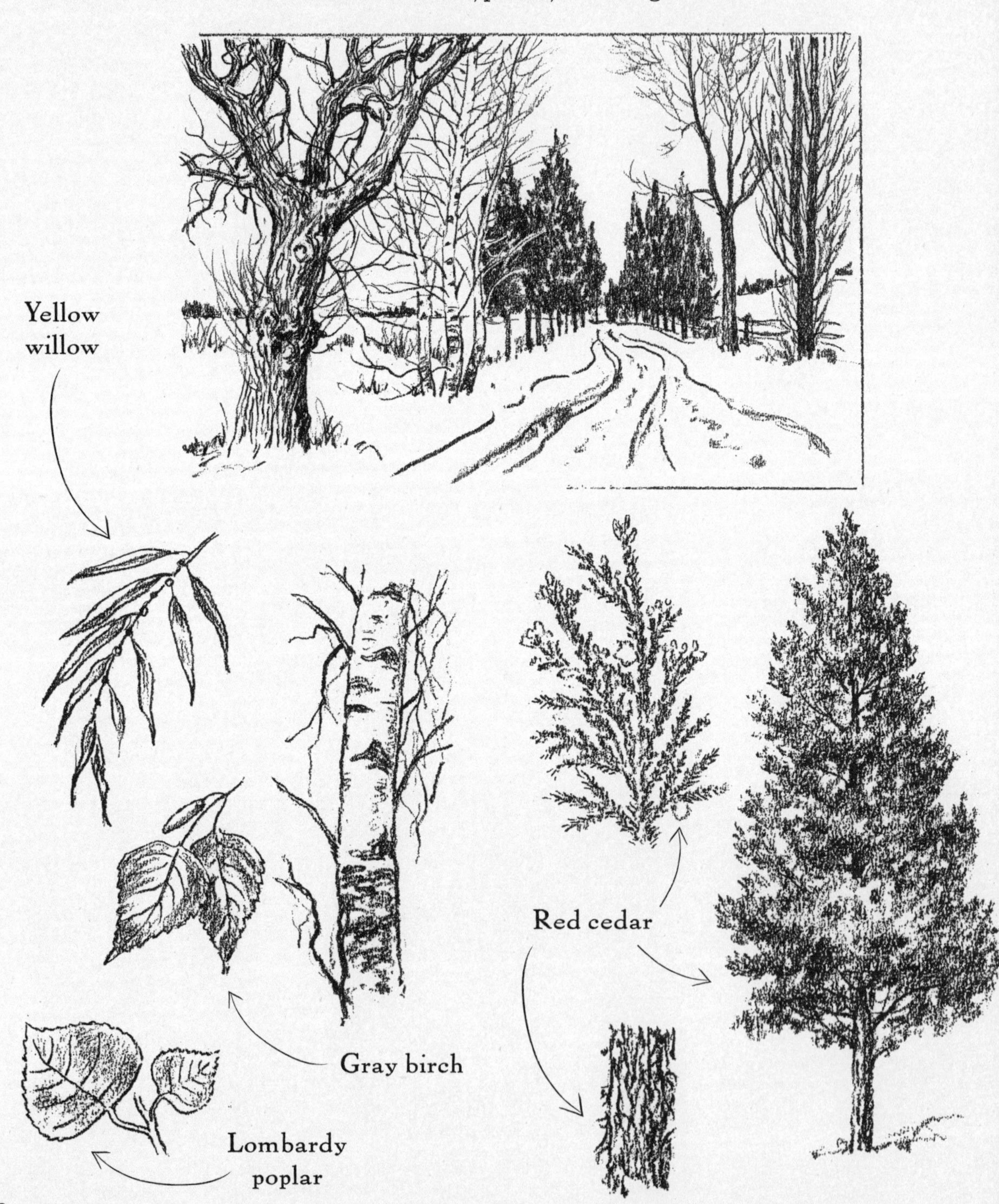

Focusing on Outline

This sketch took 15 minutes to complete and shows a simple, loose approach to outlining the masses within a scene.

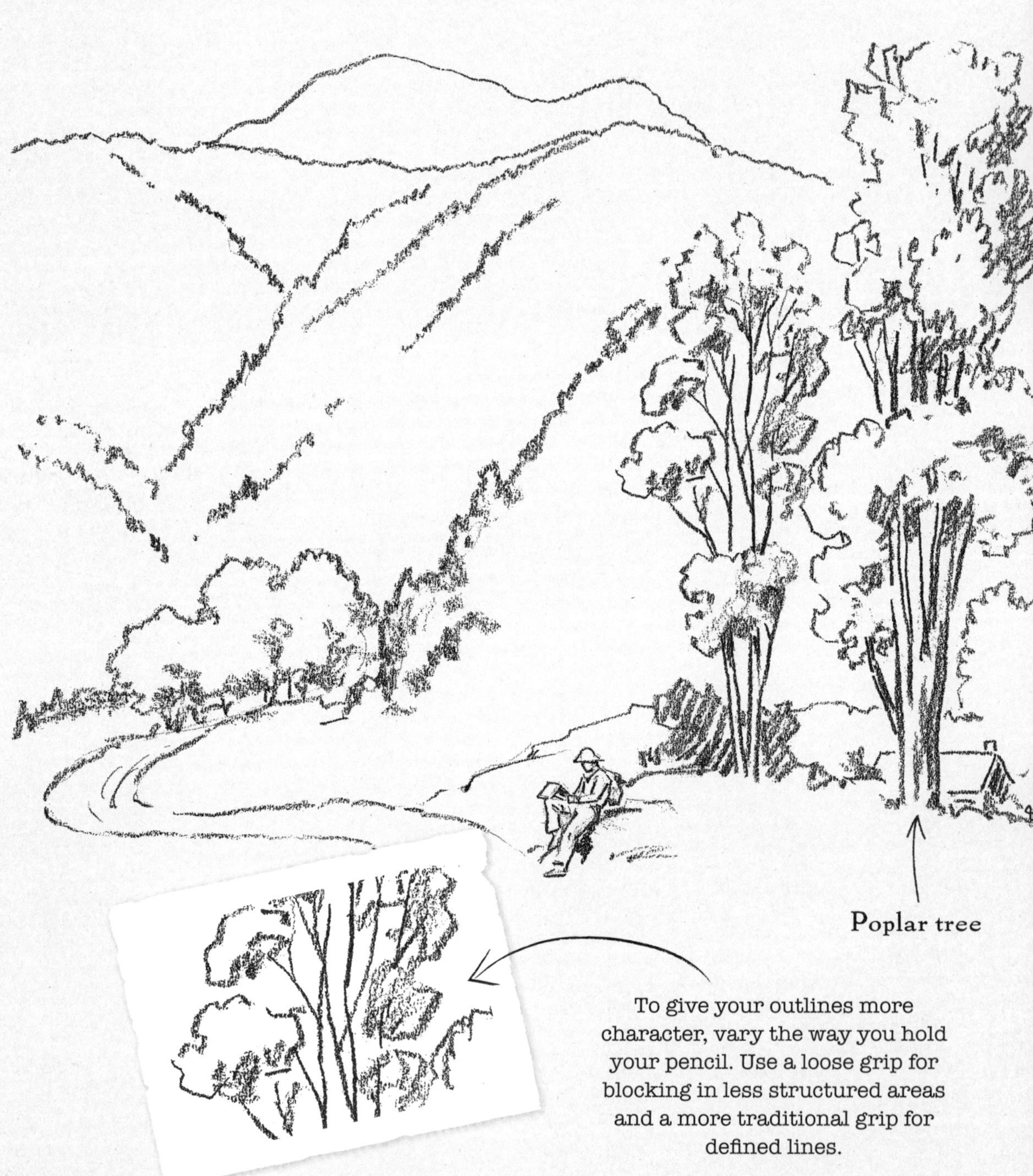

To give your outlines more character, vary the way you hold your pencil. Use a loose grip for blocking in less structured areas and a more traditional grip for defined lines.

Jersey Pine

The Jersey, or scrub, pine is a picturesque tree. A low tree with hanging branches and gray-green leaves. It grows on sterile rocky slopes of the eastern US.

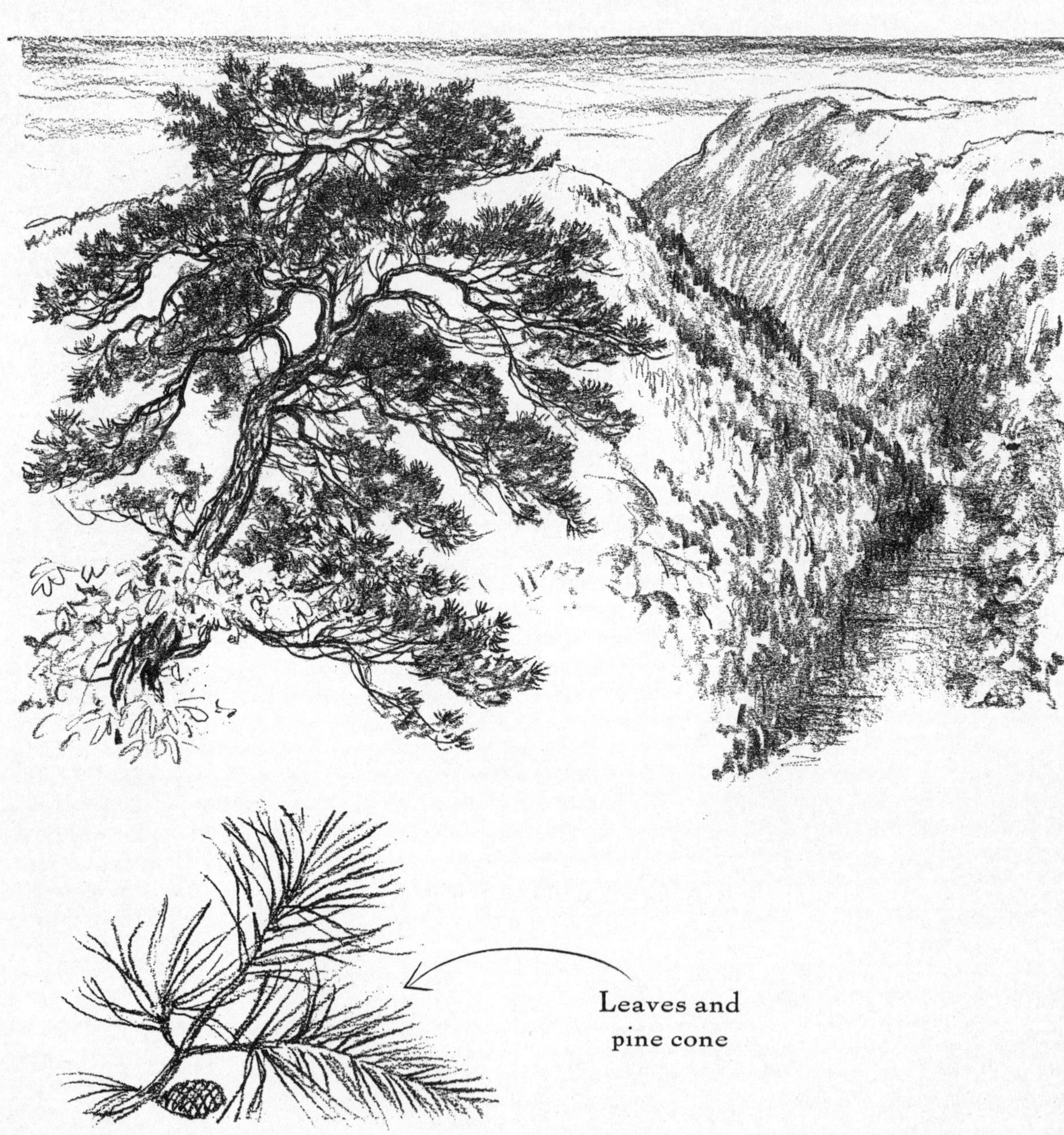

Capturing Movement

This sketch of coconut trees is a study in movement. Artists who can pick out the essential lines quickly are better equipped to capture fleeting scenes, such as these bending trees in strong wind.

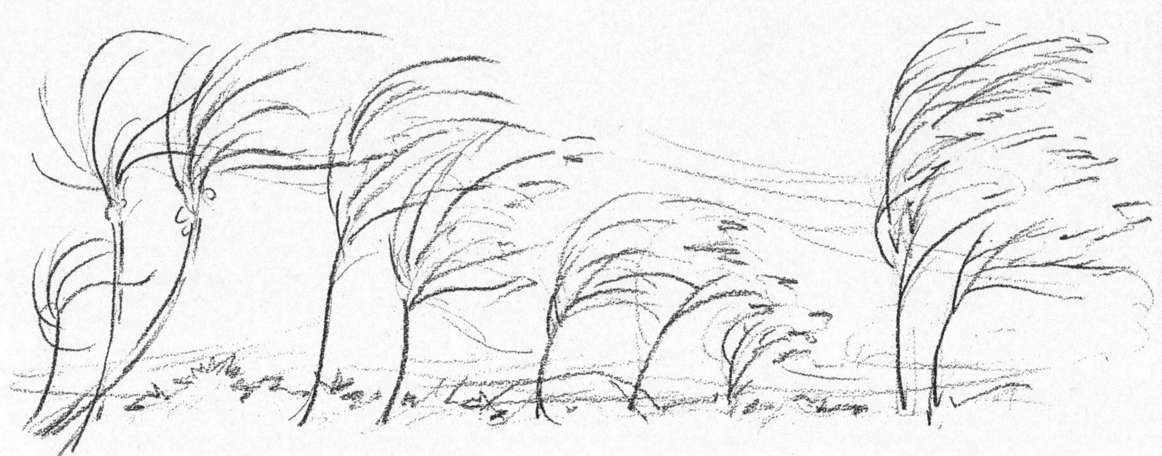

Capture the main lines as quickly as you can while communicating the flow of movement.

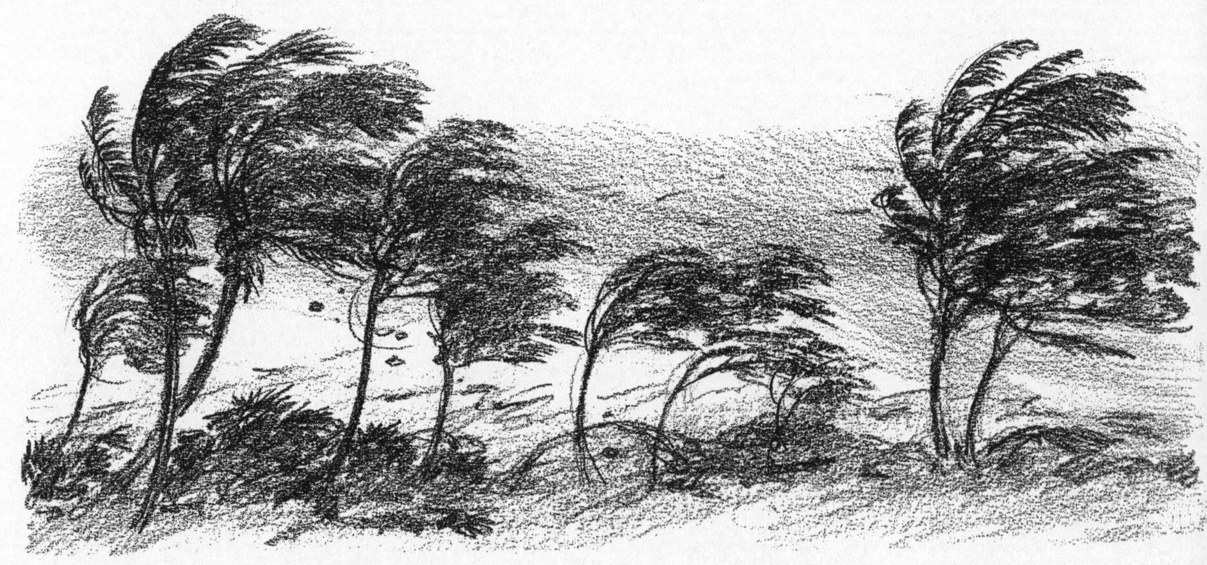

Think about the direction of each mark as you place it, stroking it in the direction of the wind.

Flora of Florida

Florida is home to the cabbage palm, coconut palms, cacti, palmetto, and many other trees and shrubs indigenous to the South, which give a strikingly unique appearance to the Southern landscapes.

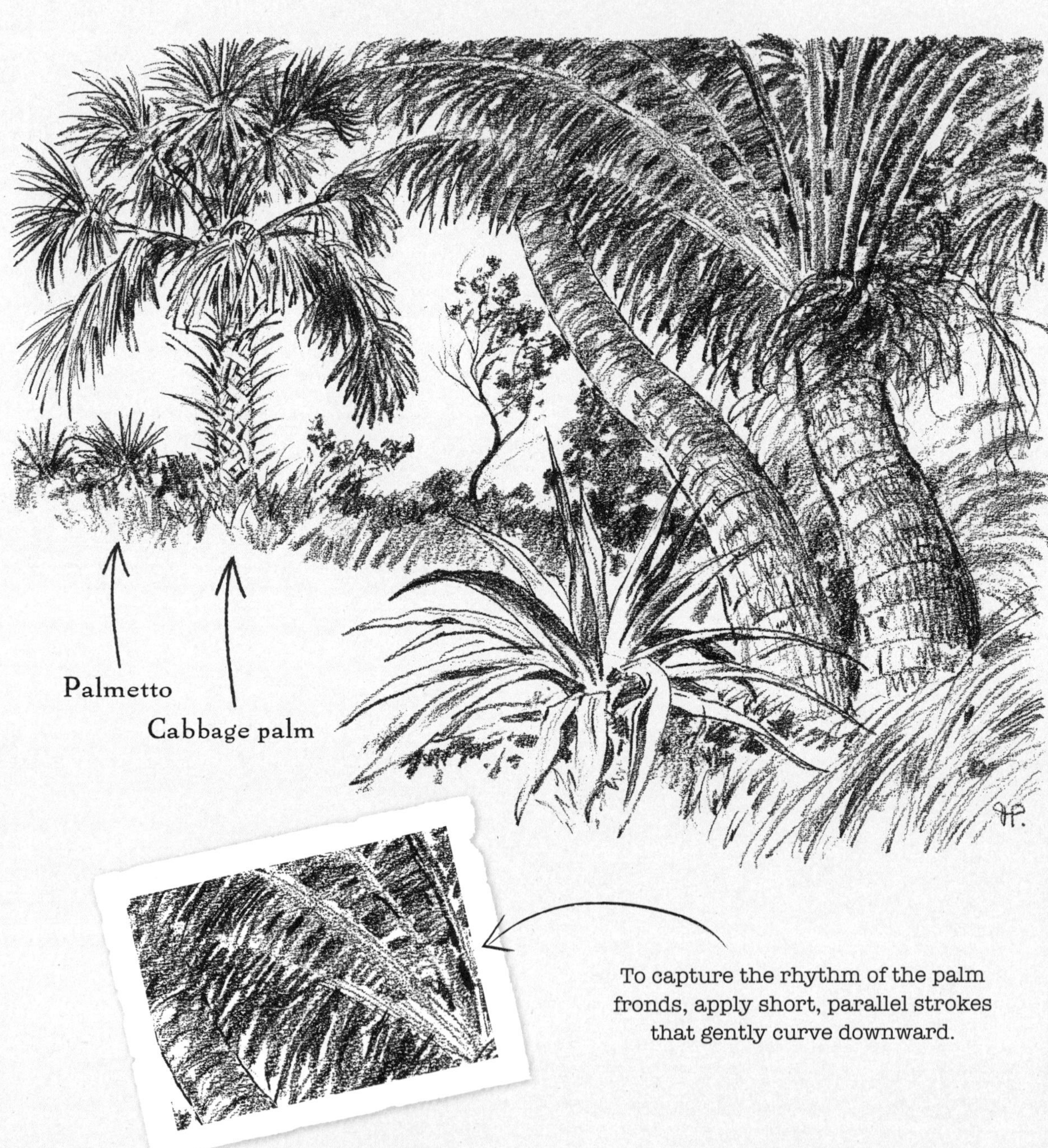

To capture the rhythm of the palm fronds, apply short, parallel strokes that gently curve downward.

The Giant Trees of California

Sequoia Trees

The sequoia is the largest evergreen in the world. It can grow up to 300 feet high on the slopes of the Sierra Nevada Mountains.

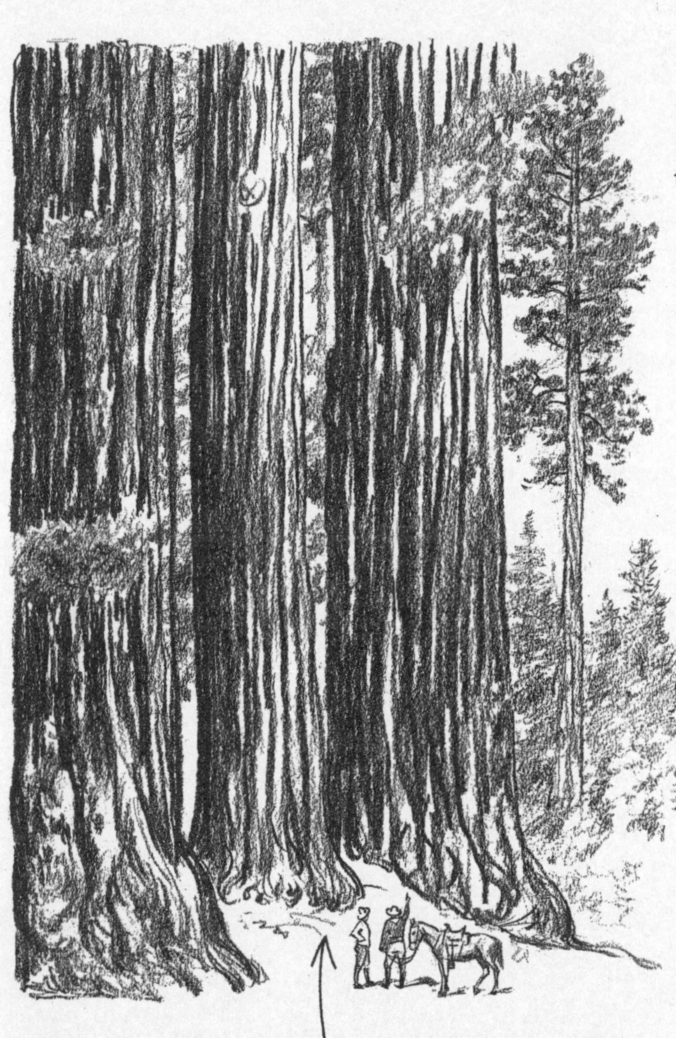

Redwood Trees

Giant redwoods can be found from Oregon down to the California coastal ranges. They flourish even at an elevation of 2,500 feet. These majestic trees are the remains of an ancient group that survived the glacial period.

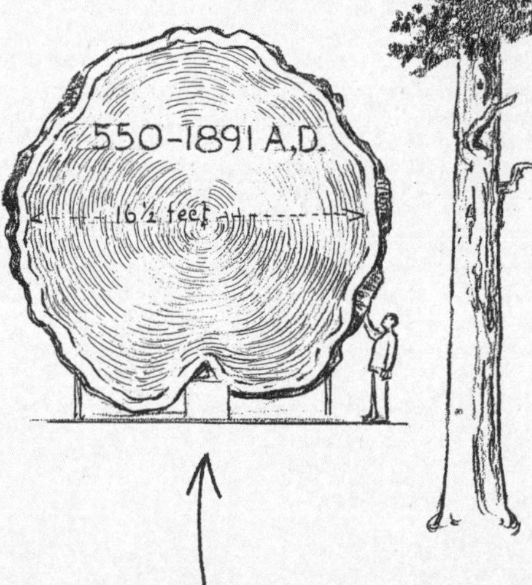

This tree lived to be 1,341 years old. Some forty generations of people lived and died during that time.

White Birch

Native to the Northern Hemisphere, white birch trees add charm to the shores of lakes and streams. They are well-suited for a free, sketchy approach to drawing.

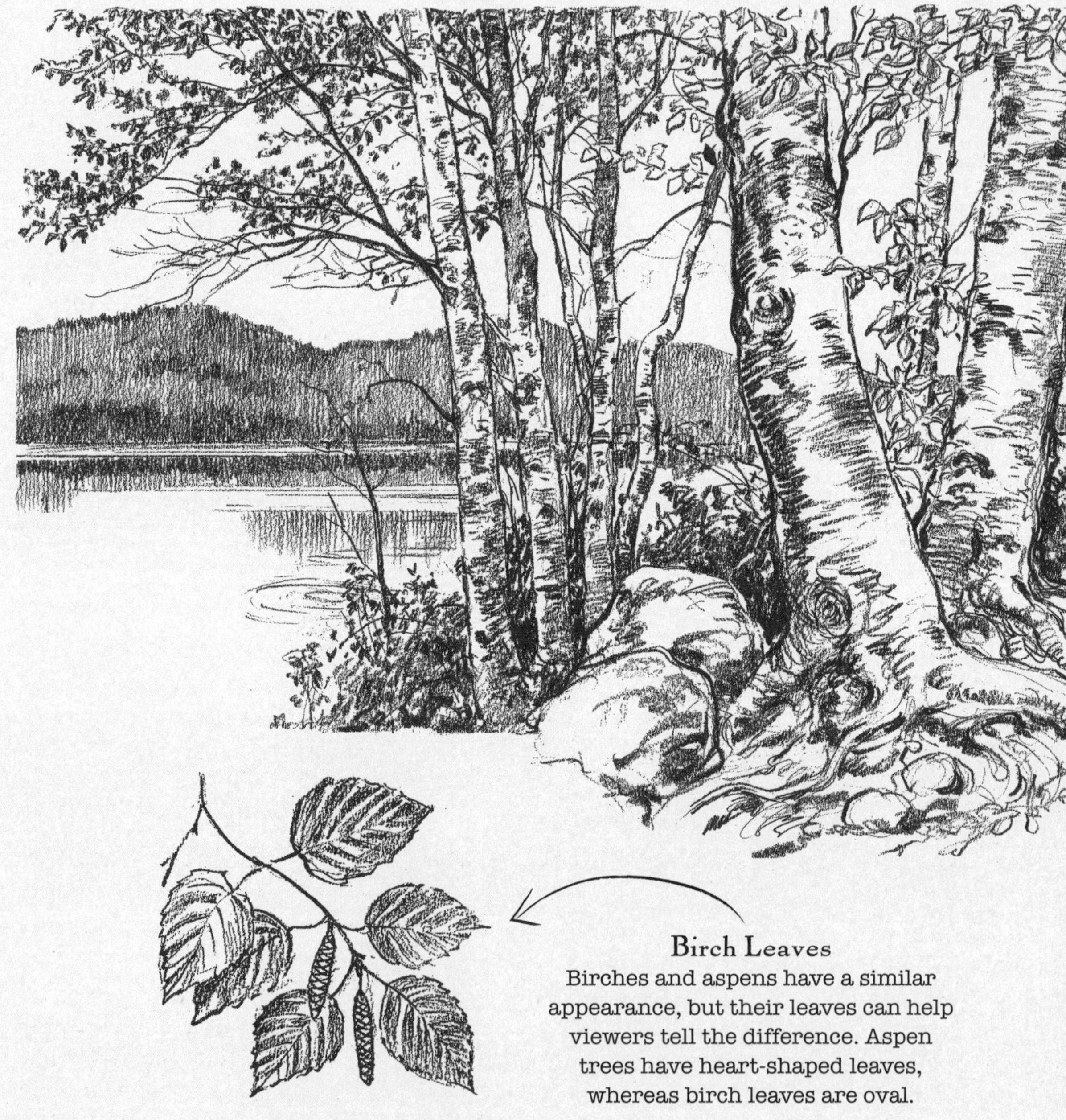

Birch Leaves

Birches and aspens have a similar appearance, but their leaves can help viewers tell the difference. Aspen trees have heart-shaped leaves, whereas birch leaves are oval.

Rugged Landscapes

Along an unprotected mountain ridge, an old sentinel has been uprooted by winter blasts. Its companion, the old pine, has suffered the mutilation of broken branches. Rough, confident strokes are ideal for representing these survivors of windswept, rugged terrain.

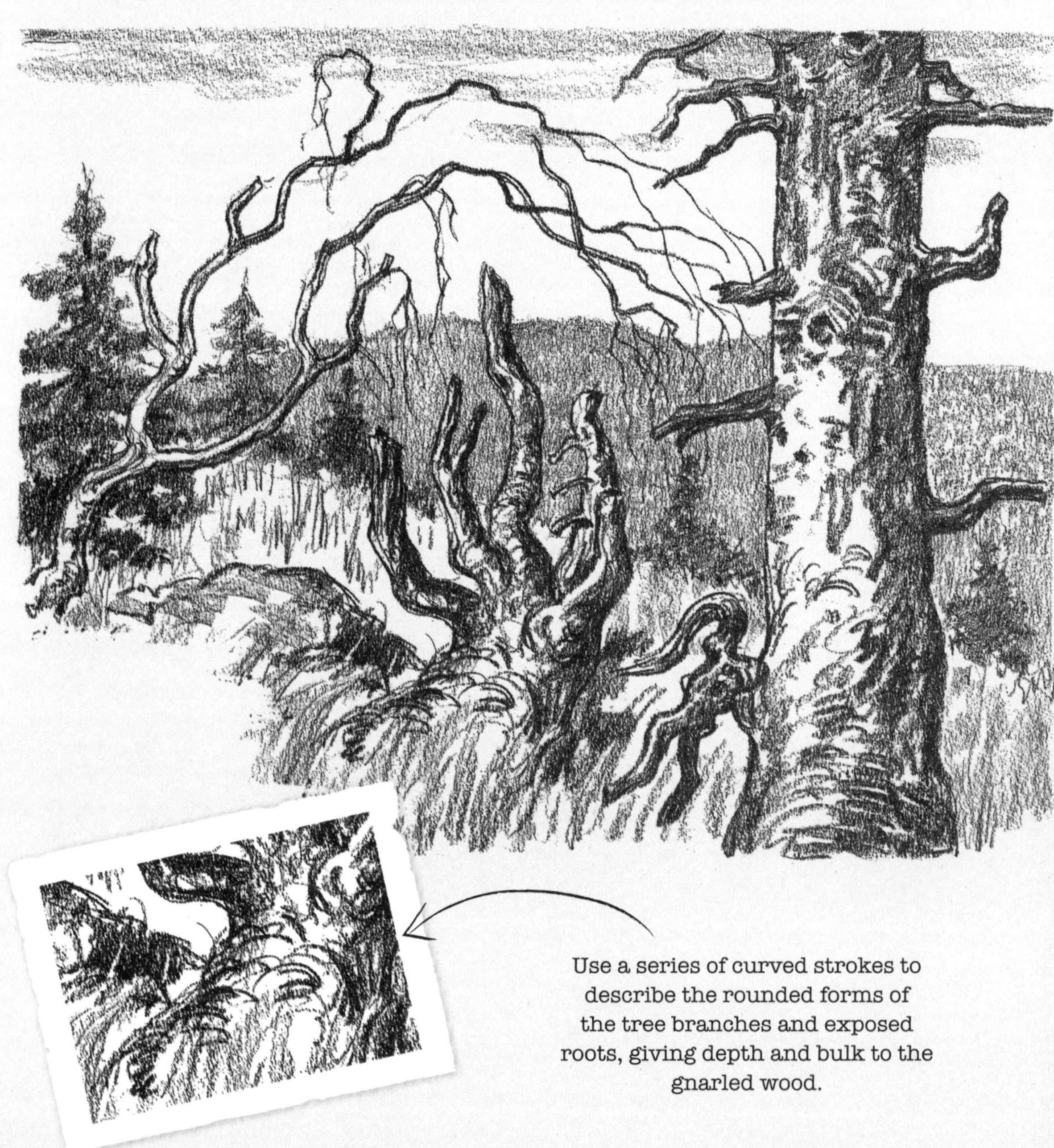

Use a series of curved strokes to describe the rounded forms of the tree branches and exposed roots, giving depth and bulk to the gnarled wood.

White Pine

The white pine is the tallest pine in the northeastern areas of the US. It rises from 50 to 150 feet in height and has a straight trunk with tapering, wide-spreading branches. Of the graceful white pine, Henry David Thoreau once wrote, “There is no finer tree.”

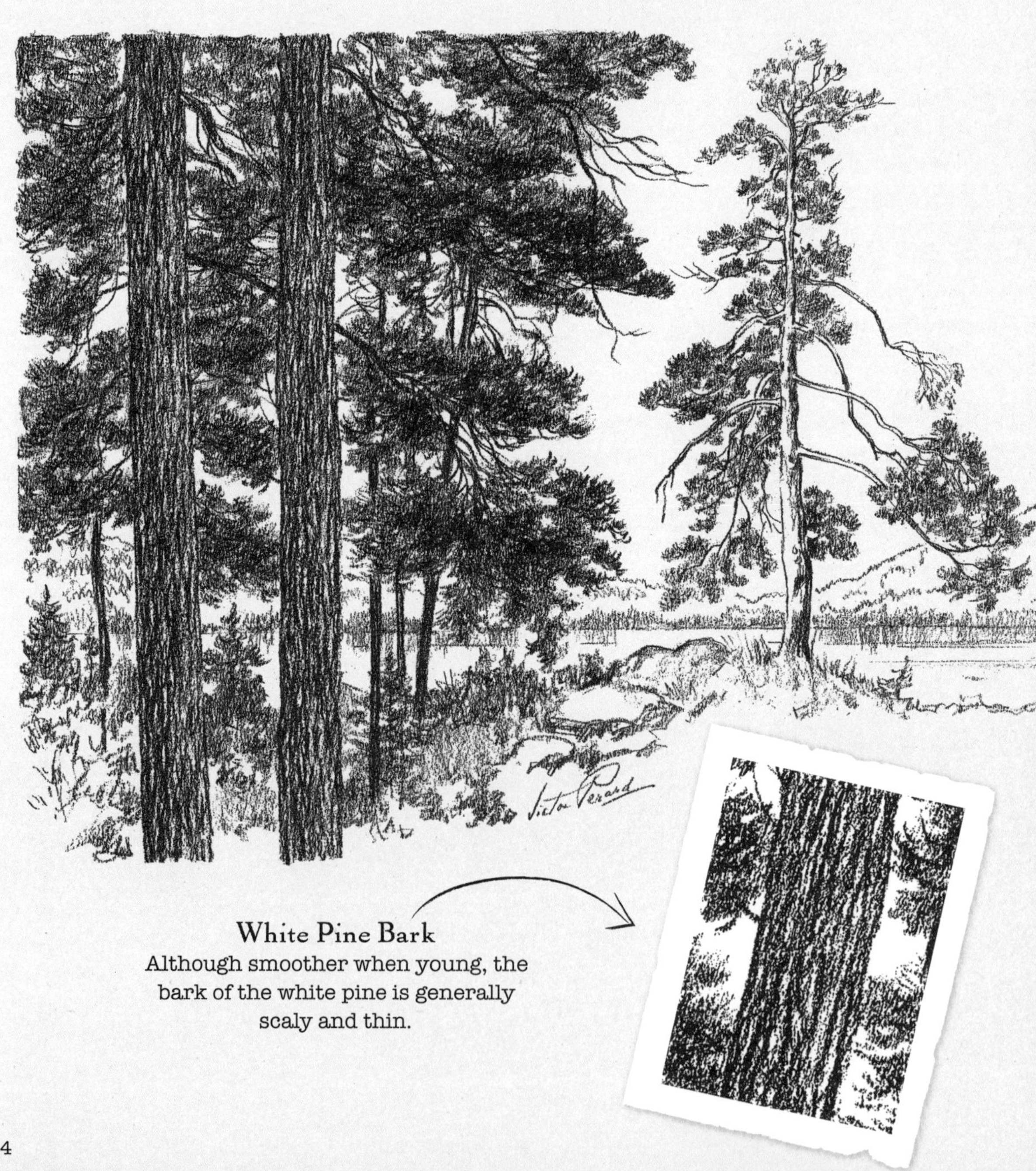

White Pine Bark

Although smoother when young, the bark of the white pine is generally scaly and thin.

White Pine Roots

This sketch shows the exposed roots of a white pine, completed at Schroon Lake in the Adirondack Mountains. The waters of the lake, at times varying in height, have washed away the earth from the roots. These show the struggle to find nourishment for a large tree.

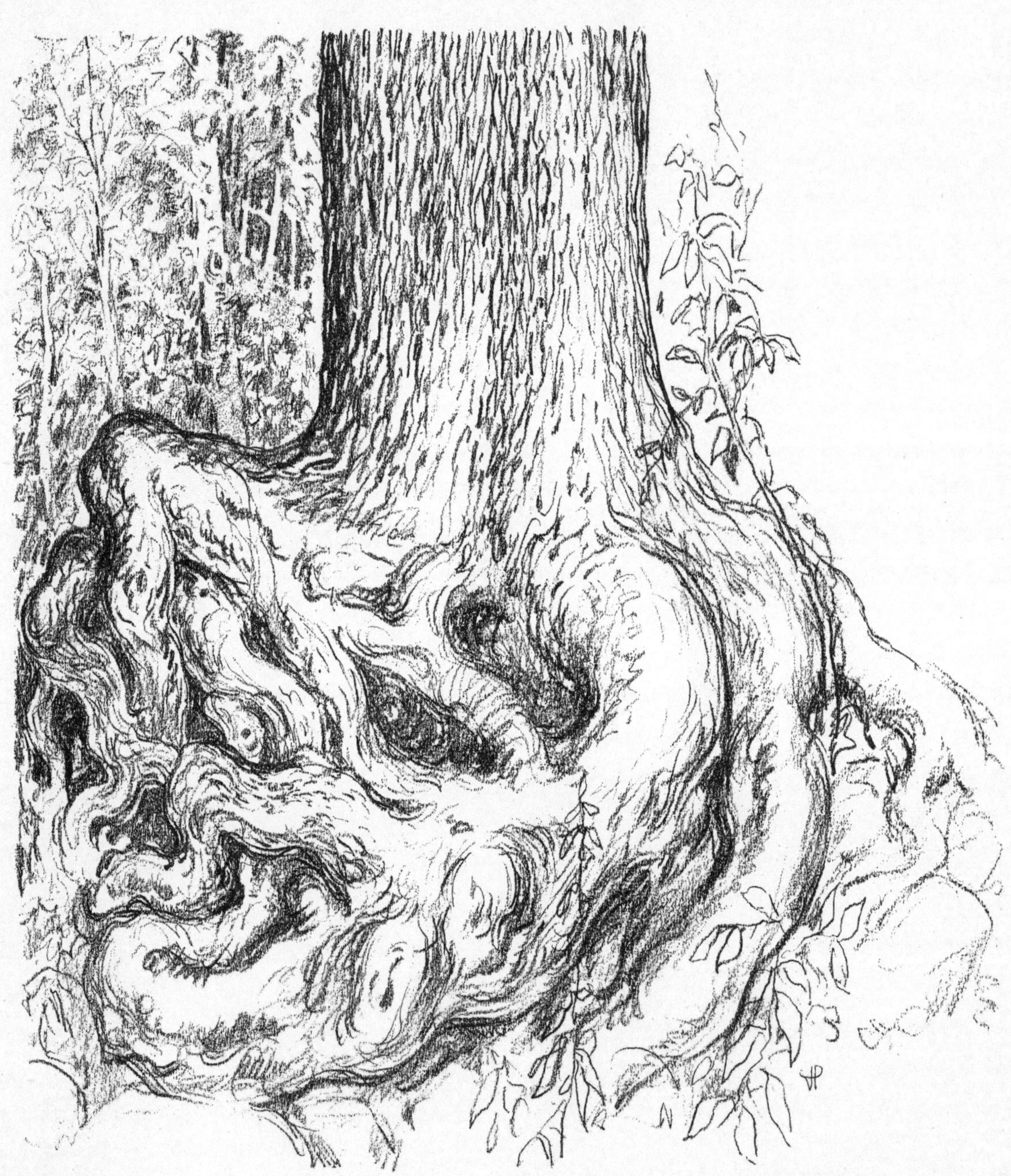

White Pine Branching

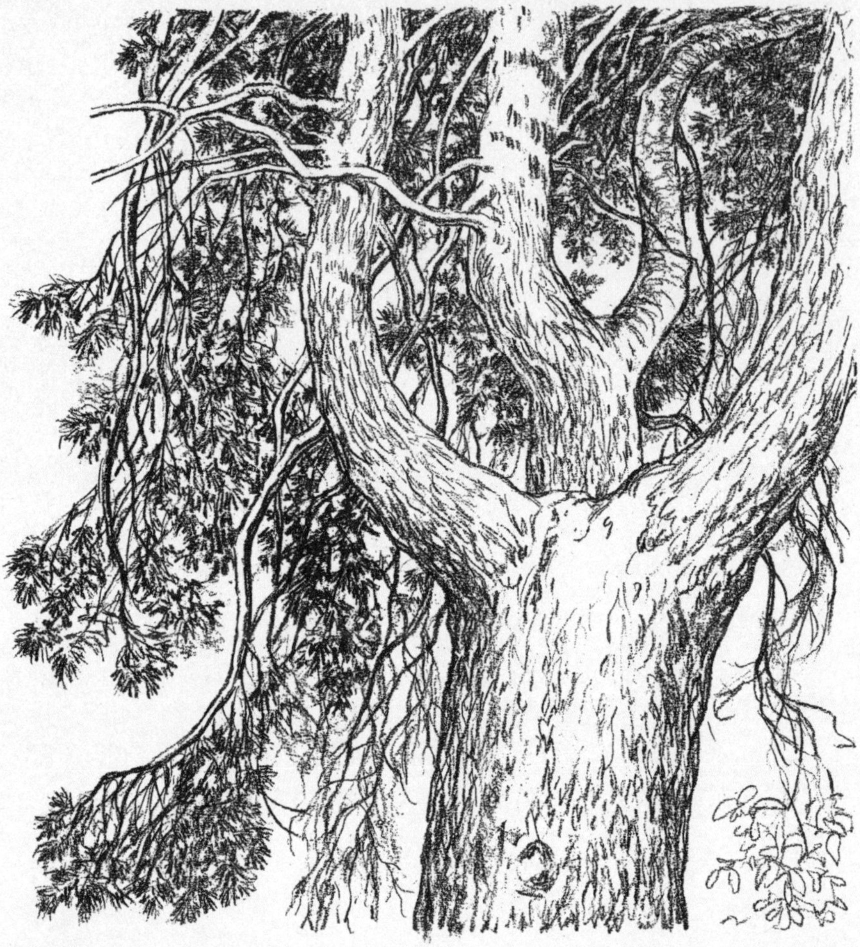

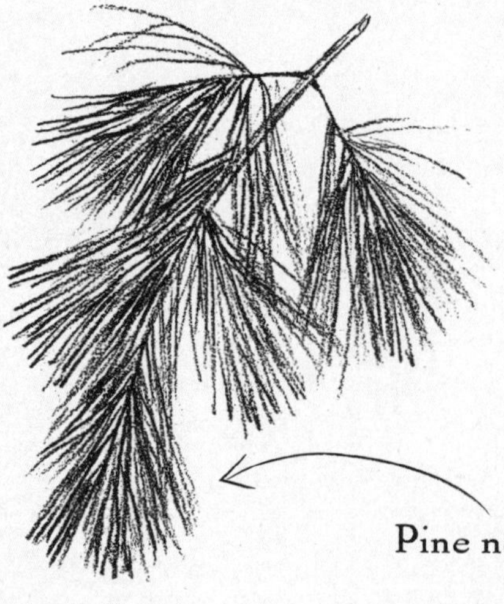

This gnarled old white pine presents a picturesque appearance, but it's of little value as lumber. The tree shown here must have had its leader branch killed by insects at a young age. Three erect limbs have taken the place of what otherwise would have been a straight tree.

Pine needles

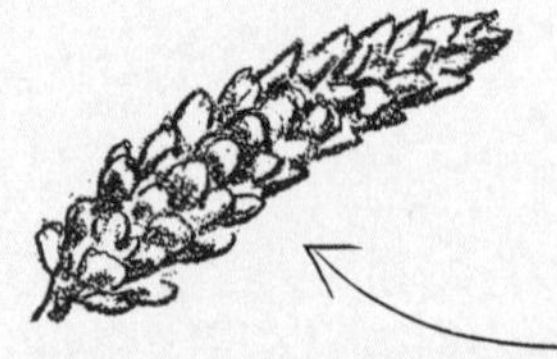

Pine cone

Oak Tree

Oak species vary quite a bit in leaf shape, but they are all hardy trees with deep roots. Their branches take abrupt changes of direction and are full of vital strength.

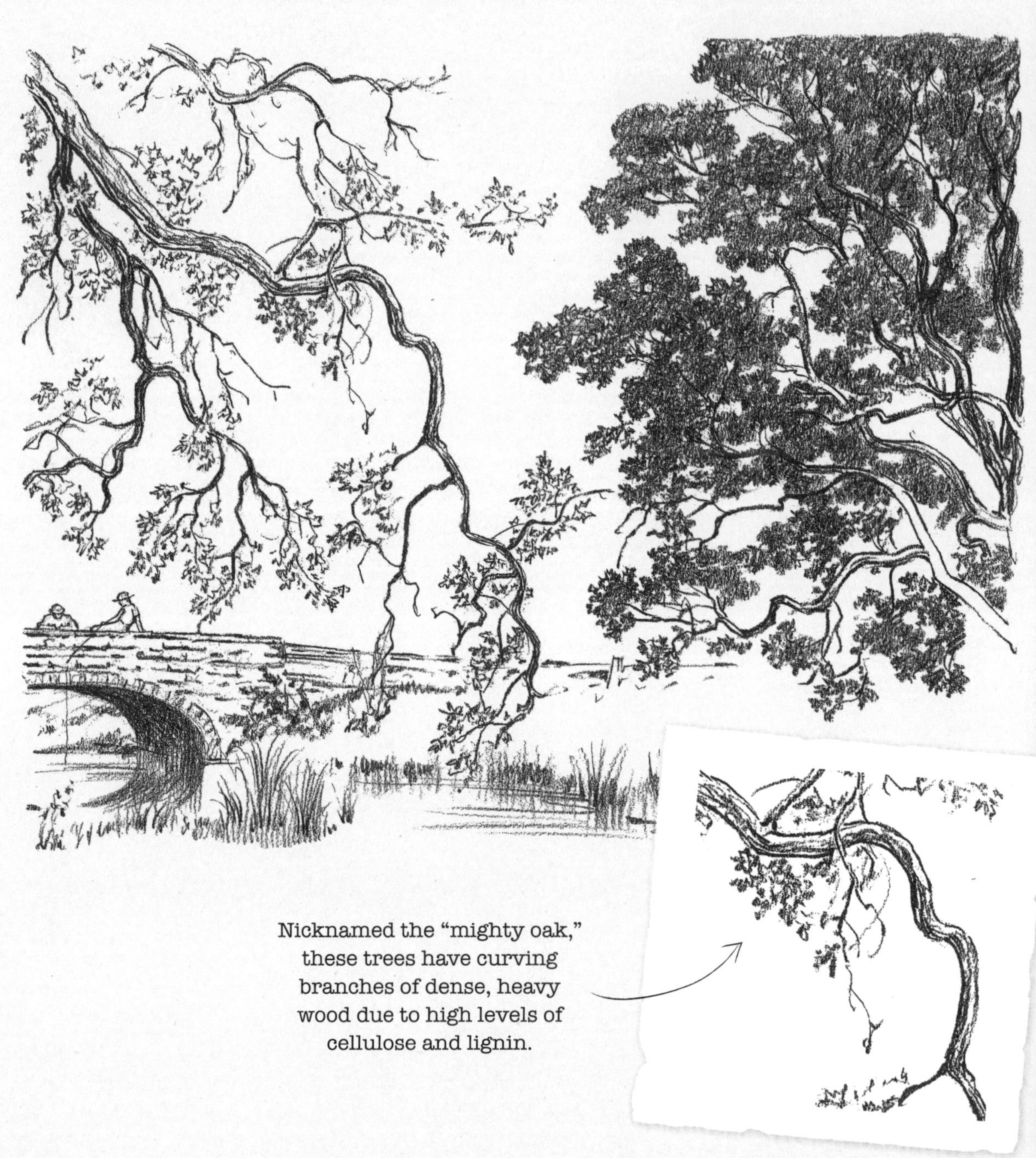

Nicknamed the "mighty oak," these trees have curving branches of dense, heavy wood due to high levels of cellulose and lignin.

Basket Willow

The basket willow (or osier willow) is a large tree that can reach 60 feet in height. It generally leans to one side, with a number of spreading branches low on the trunk. The bark is deeply furrowed.

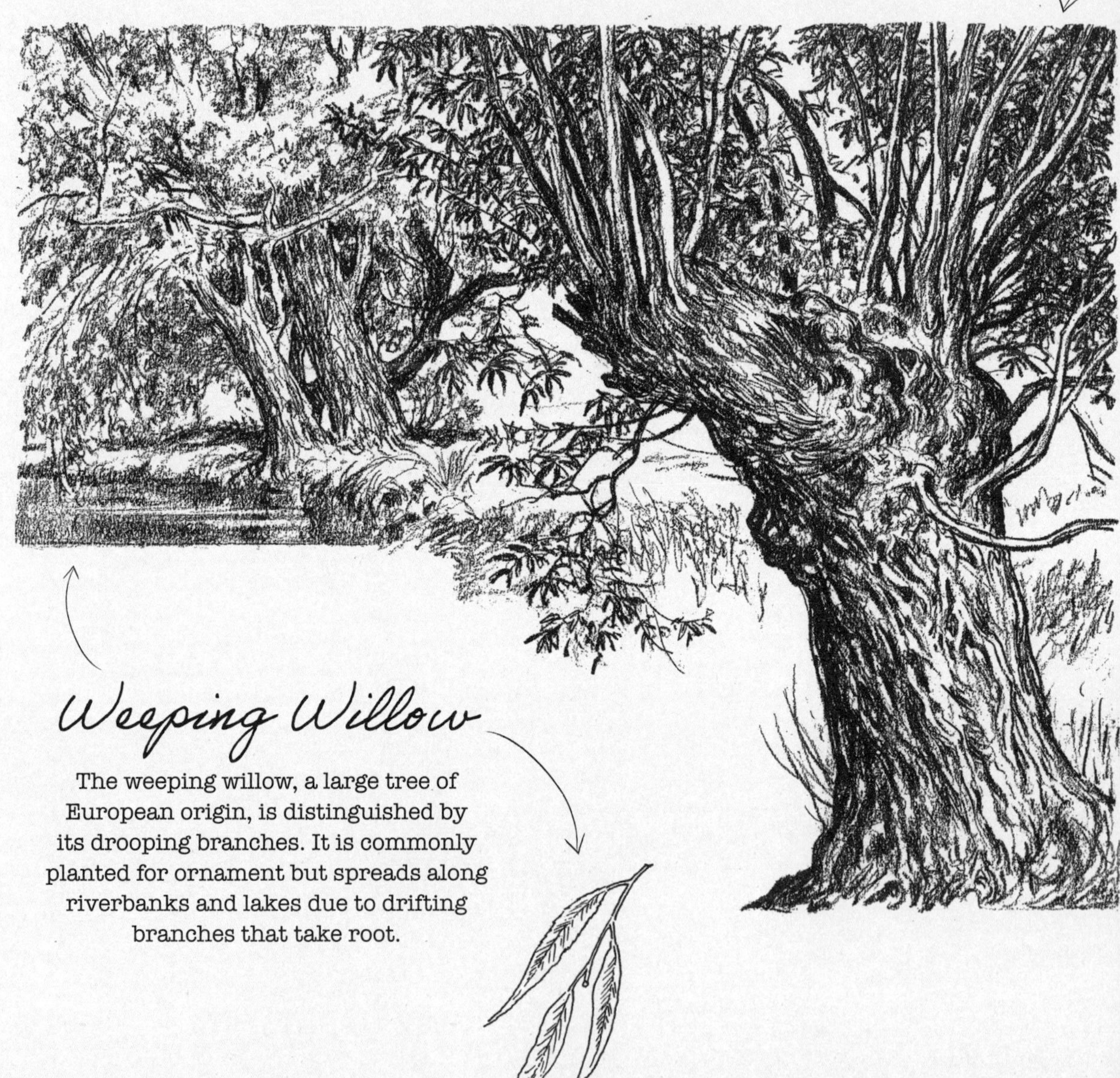

Weeping Willow

The weeping willow, a large tree of European origin, is distinguished by its drooping branches. It is commonly planted for ornament but spreads along riverbanks and lakes due to drifting branches that take root.

Golden Willows

Golden willows seem to enjoy being close to the sea. They help to grace the town of Provincetown on Cape Cod. In this sketch, the foliage of the trees in the distance should be kept in simple, flat tones—otherwise it will interfere with the clarity of the foreground.

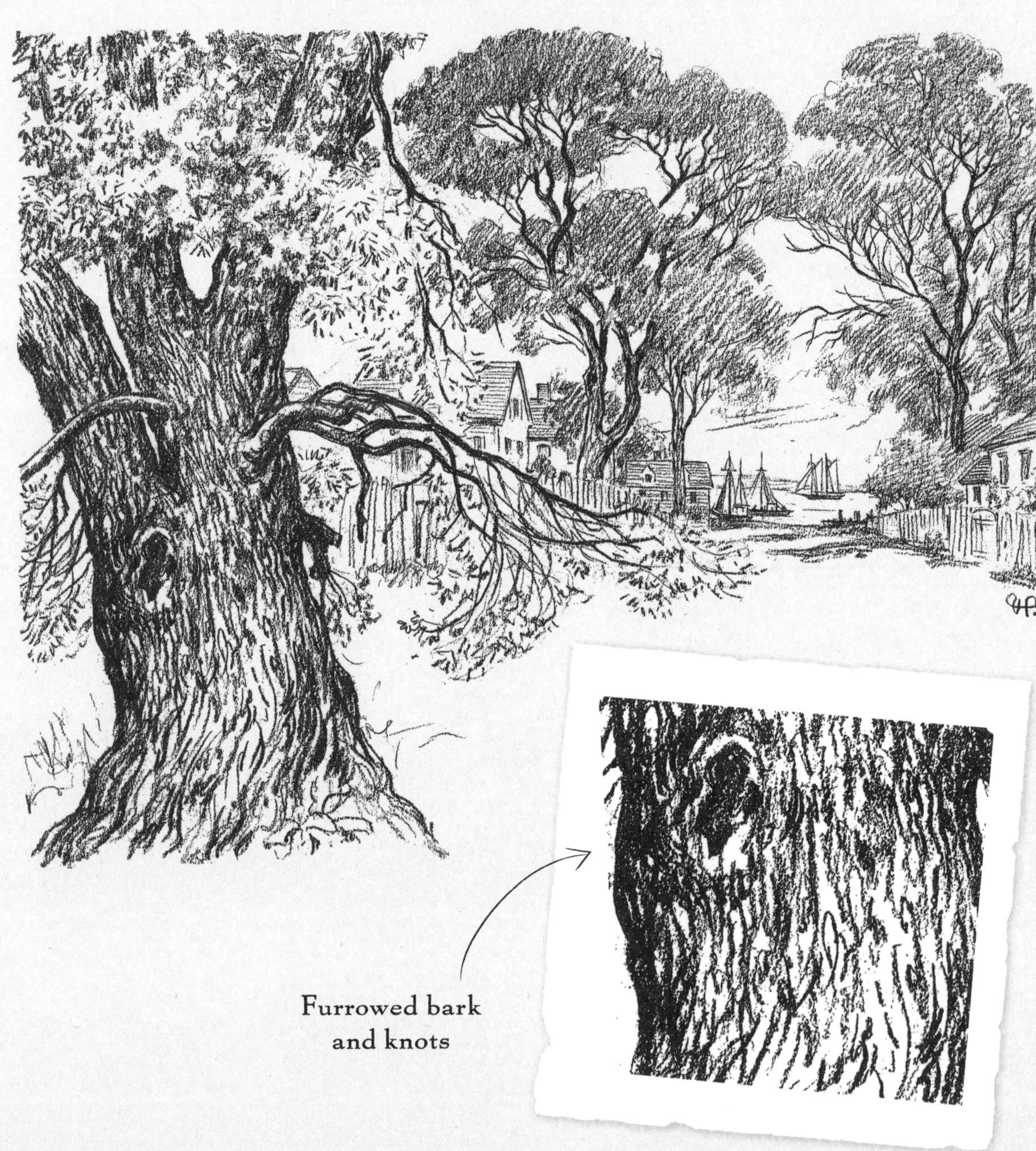

Furrowed bark and knots

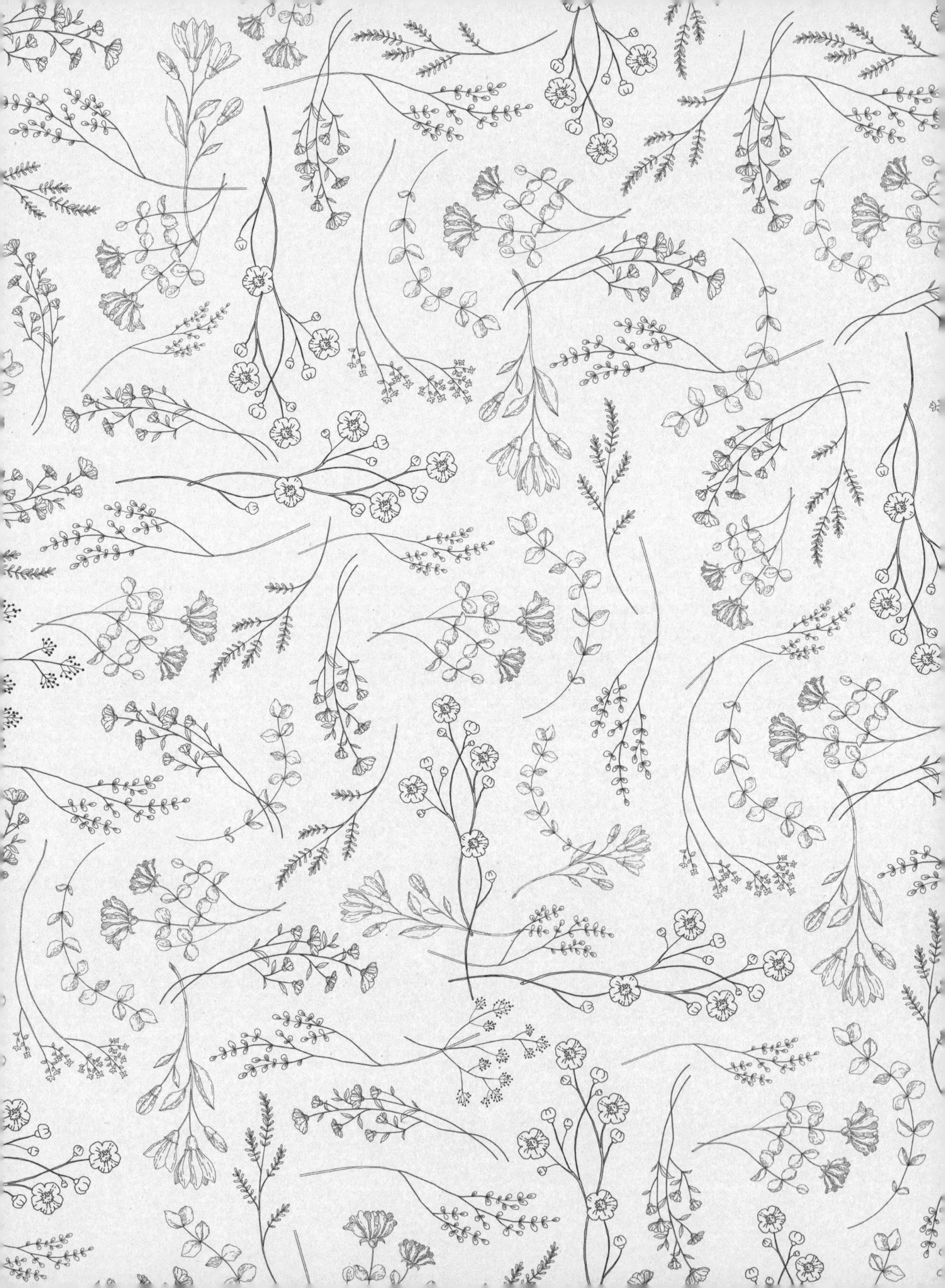

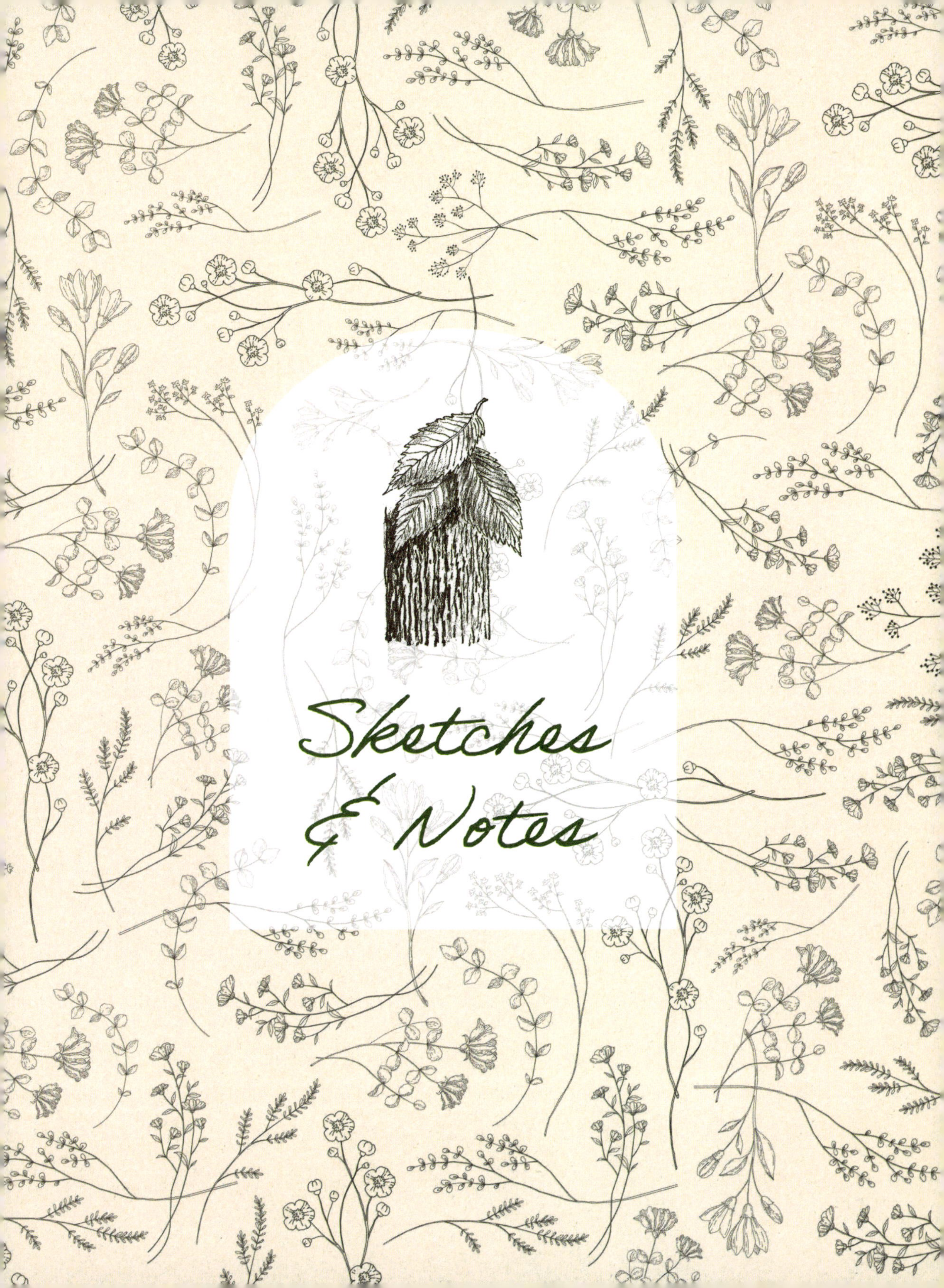
Sketches
& Notes

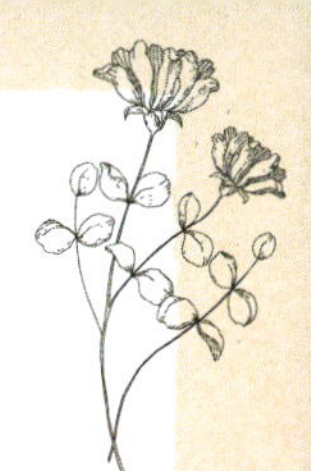

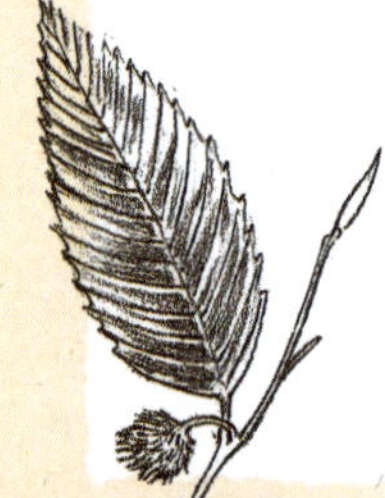

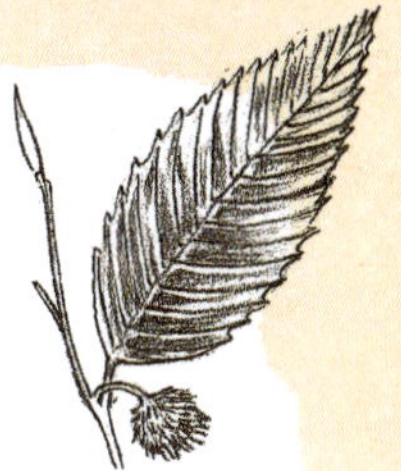

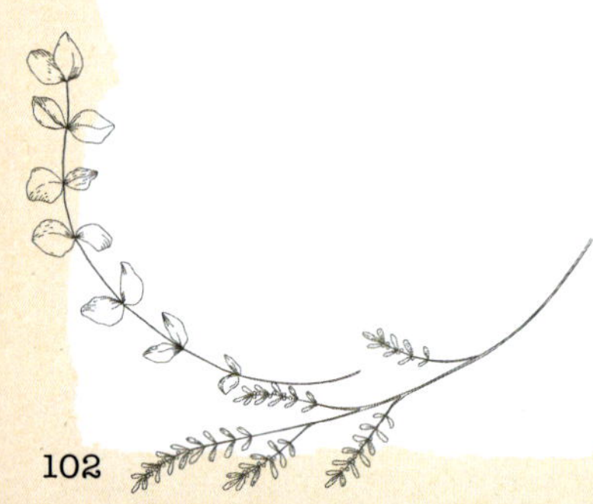

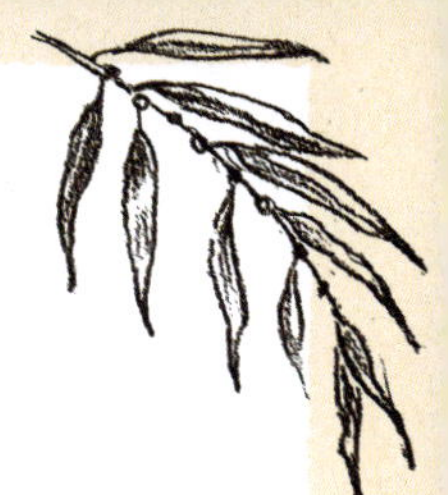

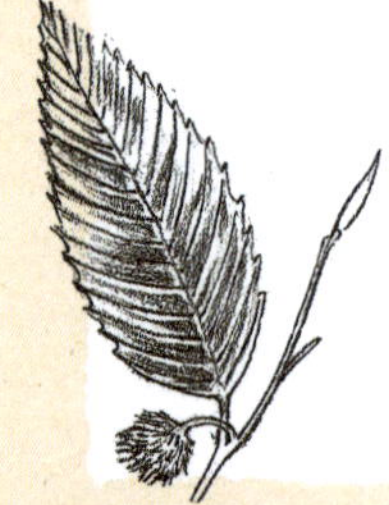

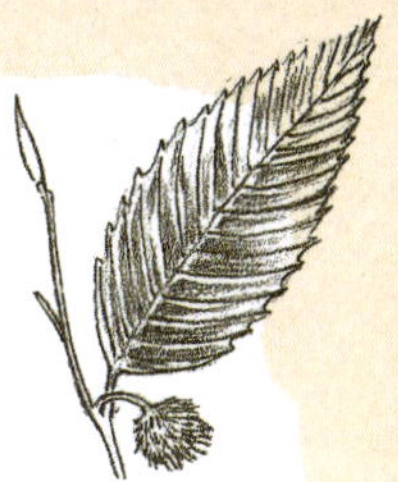

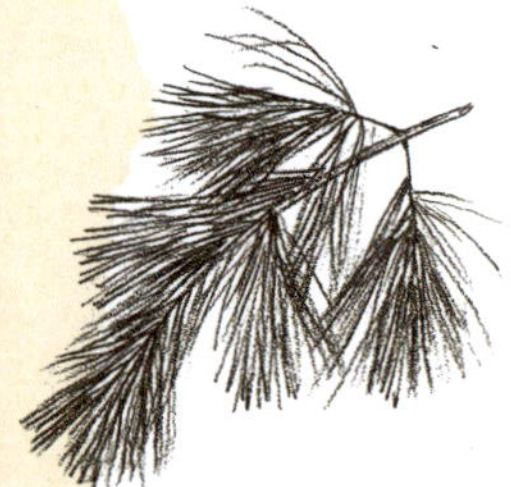

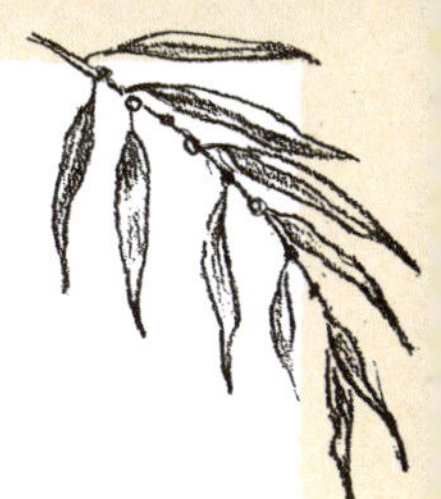

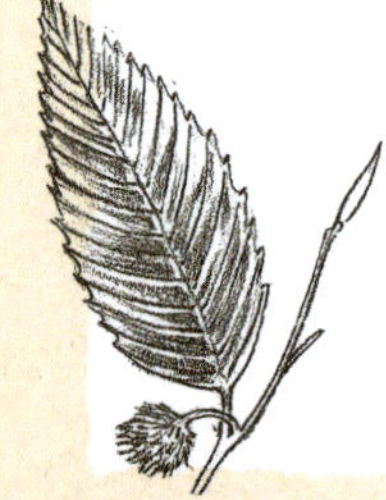

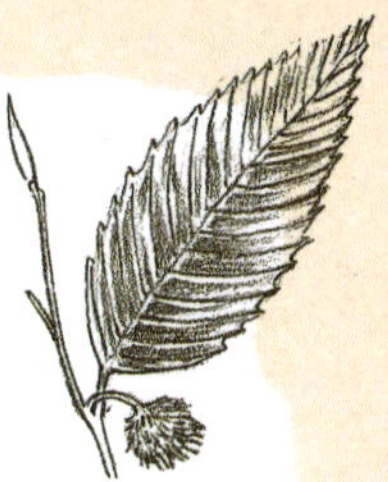

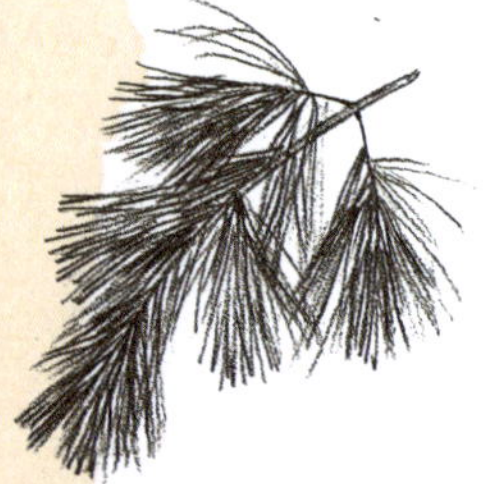

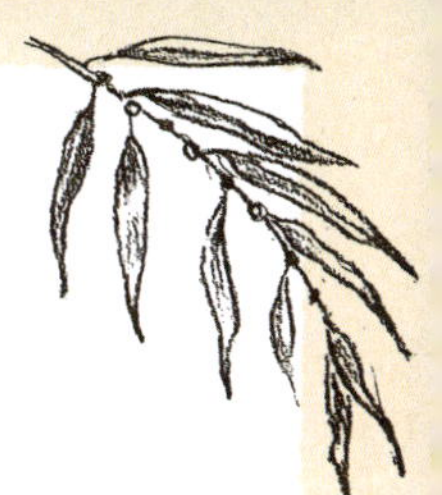

Final thoughts...